MINDFUL MASCULINITY WORKBOOK

This book belongs to:

_____

This book is dedicated to the women and men
who have shaped and inspired me
to be the man I am today.

My wife, Tricia, thank you for giving me the space to
fail and for patiently loving me as I grow.

My twin sister, Anastasia, without you I wouldn't exist.
There are no words to describe your impact in my life.

My mom for working hard to support our family and my dad
for staying home with us and modeling a non-traditional masculinity.
My aunt for inspiring fearlessness.

The Smith Family, for modeling stability, gentleness and kindness.

My guardian angels, Alexis and Wickie.

My brothers and co-conspirators in creating Camp Lost Boys.
C.M., thank you for supporting and pushing me
into this next chapter of life's work and for modeling
dignified masculinity.

TABLE OF CONTENTS

INTRODUCTION

Greetings, fellow men and masculine-identified people!

I'm so happy that you've arrived here. If you're anything like me—and I'll assume some similarity, since you picked up a book on scrutinizing your masculinity—then you're ready to become a better guy. That is a radical first step. And this book will put you on the path to becoming the man you wish to be.

Maybe you're wondering what the hell "mindful masculinity" is, anyway. Plainly put, it entails bringing a new level of intentionality and awareness to your maleness. Most people on the planet don't give much thought to their gender in any radical or transformative way. But we're living in a moment when the cultural zeitgeist demands that men be better without giving us so much as a clue how to do that. Being mindful about your masculinity is a positive and personal approach to this big cultural problem. Mindful masculinity simply means that *you* define what kind of man or masculine person you want to be and that you do so with intention and thoughtfulness.

My desire for you is that you connect to yourself as a man or masculine person; deepen that relationship; and consider what your masculinity means in the context of patriarchy. For some of you, this may be the first time you've ever thought about your gender, its expression, and the specific privileges that you've been afforded as a man or masculine person. You will learn to identify and bring awareness to your masculinity. This may be brand new and feel scary or daunting. Don't worry—we'll do it together. I won't lie, it's hard but very necessary work. Men of all levels of introspection and awareness will find something transformational about doing this work of consciously identifying and bringing awareness to their masculinity. Ideally, we should all be working on ourselves, growing, evolving and changing continuously over our entire lifetimes. This is just a beginning.

Many books have come out in recent years that have skillfully and globally put masculinity under a microscope (and some of their writers have contributed to this workbook). This is not one of them, though it has been informed by many of them. This isn't a book of diagnosis or abstract discourse. I won't spend hundreds of pages exploring the underlying problems with men. We can simply acknowledge that masculinity is in crisis now and has basically always been in crisis. Ours is nothing new.

What is new is the language, the tools and the platforms we can access on a minute-to-minute basis to send out signals the world over and sound the alarm about how shit men are. Another essential, nameable difference of this current movement versus those of the past is that we no longer give men the room to fail. If you fuck up, that's a wrap. We tell men they are broken without offering any solutions for how to fix themselves. We tell them they are obsolete trash. We cancel them. Truly, this cancel culture does a poor job of allowing people who make mistakes to learn from them.

So this workbook is a corrective. It was created as a safe space for men to fail, to try different things, reflect, stretch ourselves beyond our previous limits, and flex our capacity for compassionate change. Whatever answers you come up with to the questions in here are not wrong. You are not wrong. Your maleness or masculinity is not wrong. You are okay as you are right now, but you can always improve. And the only way to get right with yourself in your masculinity is to be honest about it.

Let me share some of my own honest story with you. My journey with masculinity was a rocky road, along which I could take nothing for granted. As a man of transgender experience, I've had a unique path to maleness that forced on me as much as it blessed me with a special lens onto gendered dynamics. From the outset, I couldn't but constantly inspect my maleness in the larger context of the world, and I still do. I have had to be intentional with my male identity and deliberate about how I occupy space.

Having spent some time in the world as a visibly queer person, I haven't always been valued in the way able-bodied, cisgender white men are typically prized by society. I wasn't born into male privilege. Rather I arrived late and, subsequently, it never sat well with me. Because of that, I can't help but notice when there's only one female manager working at the company where I'm working. I can't quietly walk by while men casually sexually harass women. I can't sit idly or silently in a room full of men cracking jokes about how "hysterical" women can be. My desire to work in solidarity with women and gender nonconforming people is integral to my sense of healthy masculinity. By no means is this true of all transgender men, nor is it untrue of all cisgender men. But whatever kind of man you are, we should all have the opportunity to learn and grow, lest we risk staying stunted and trapped in a system that hurts people of all gender identities and experiences.

If you are a cis man reading this and thinking, *there is no way a trans guy could teach me anything about being a man,* I say to you: There is no way a trans guy *can't* teach you a ton about being a man! One of the core ideas I hope each person holding this book takes from it is that you can learn to be a healthy man from any person, regardless of gender. Listening with an open mind and remaining flexible to learning are essential to embodying the healthy masculinity described in here. Additionally and specifically, though trans men and cis men have different paths to maleness, they are men equally. *All* men are valid men. All men can and *should* teach each other how to be better, healthier men. All people should participate in this conversation about repair.

For its part, this book adds a range of remarkable voices to the conversation—but this book is not about its author or any of the other incredible contributors propounding our opinions about men and masculinity prescriptively. We are merely offering you our insights and examples as a springboard for your movement. We see this book as a partnership between ourselves and you, the reader. You have entered into an agreement by cracking it open. And by doing the work, you can actively craft your own definition of healthy masculinity, and figure out how best to embody it. The people that have generously and vulnerably lent their voices to this workbook have experienced masculinity in contexts where masculinity and patriarchy have been rigorously and even violently policed—sometimes in the most literal sense. And while the personal stories we share with you are as diverse as our gendered experiences, all of the authors in here are united behind the singular aim of getting you to think deeply and critically about your own masculinity. Even if you are already a "good man" by your own measure, we hope nonetheless that you'll seize the ensuing opportunities to go deeper, parse out your blindspots, and home in on areas of potential improvement. You *get* to become better.

The point of this approach is to side-step a major trap that many men are falling into right now, a false dichotomy pitting us between the two extremes of an emasculating fear of "toxicity," or an unsubstantiated male pride and over-the-top fetishization of (white) masculinity. To paint a picture:

lonely, keyboard-warrior incels and pseudo-sensitive hipsters high on ayahuasca, led on journeys inside to the wounded inner child by dread-locked white men in their twenties with animal pelts slung across their shoulders, war paint smeared on their faces, and Instagram followings of 100K—these are actually two sides of the same extremist coin. Both are manifestations of reactionary masculinity, and both oppose the style of responsive, responsible masculinity this workbook takes as its theme. This workbook guides you to a place where you learn to stop reacting and start responding and being responsible. You don't need to fall prey to those polemical, polarized and polarizing ideas of what makes you a man. You don't need to react defensively to what's going on in the world today. You can choose instead to define your maleness and masculinity proactively beyond the pitfalls of patriarchy.

Indeed, masculinity isn't about picking sides or doing what you think men should do. It comes down to *who you are* and how you embody your authenticity as a man, whatever that means to you. A flamboyantly gay man is as much a man as a hypermasculine Marine. A fey, transgender man is just as much a man as beefy, roid-raging gym rat. There are infinite ways to be a man. There is no wrong or right way to be any gender. Period. Full stop. It has taken nearly two decades for me to let this truth sink in and integrate itself into my being. Let me tell you about a turning point in my process getting there.

A couple of years ago, with two other transgender men, I started a summer camp for men of transgender experience called Camp Lost Boys. Although I had intended to create this camp for the benefit of other guys—not me—it was there that I realized how desperate *I* was for this space and experience, how direly *I* needed this connection to other men who traveled a similarly thoughtful path to their male identity. It was there that I realized how isolated I'd felt from other men and my own masculinity and, consequently, how I'd been harboring an old and obsolete hatred in my heart. The damaging beliefs I'd had about *all men* being toxic had corroded *my* sense of self.

I didn't consciously identify with this hate of men and self twenty years into life as an adult man in the world. I've done so much work to suss out and undo other outdated modalities and limiting beliefs I've held in my life. I've picked up tools I wasn't gifted for my own spiritual and emotional growth. Now forty years old, I've been in twelve-step programs nearly fifteen years, and therapy over twenty-five. I am firmly rooted in my desire to be the best version of myself I can be, and truly believe that others are capable of healing and feeling good in themselves, too. But these challenging feelings I had about men were blocking me from loving myself fully, from evolving and finding ways to channel my energy positively into solving the real enemy my heart was confusing with "all men": patriarchal masculinity.

So I started considering the linguistic terrain we've settled on as a culture to map out the changes it demands in men and masculinity; in other words, what language we use to describe the problem and ostensibly solve it. It struck me, the ever-present conversation about "toxic masculinity" we hear today can feel unnuanced and overgeneralized. The current deployment of the term "toxic" tends to be used uncritically and irreproachably, as a stopgap to curb productive dialogue and put masculinity beyond the pale. Men are left to unpack the problem with themselves on their own, with too few follow-up discussions in search of potential solutions. Toxicity requires a hazmat suit and a special trash can for untouchable waste; it feels tainted beyond repair. I don't know about you, but I need to see more possibility, more potential for redemption, in the very language we use to interact with the issues at hand.

That's why I'm reframing so-called toxicity as "problematic masculinity." "Problematic" still acknowledges the need for correction while holding onto hope and begging for solution. After all, men themselves are not radioactive refuse. *Patriarchy* is the toxic waste that needs disposing, and men need to play a hands-on role in taking out the trash. Men ought not only listen to others but learn about the toxicity others detect and call out in male culture. And then men need to be able to spot those stumbling blocks themselves, so they can come together with the culture and carve out fresh, progressive pathways past the problem of patriarchy. (The only way out is through!) In short, men need to stop opting to be victims of circumstance and start choosing to become active agents of positive change today. The realization I had about myself at camp helped me get unstuck from my own unproductive negativity and steered me in this connective, reparative direction with my masculinity. What you're reading right now is the proof of that re-route: a roadmap for anybody, plotted by me and fellow-travelers in mindful masculinity, to lead us all from hate to love and healing.

That's the mission of this workbook—to inspire more love. Self love. Love for others. Love for the challenging universal experience of being a person in the world. My highest desire for this project is to send healing love to masculinity. The vague hate I felt suffusing my own male experience and men generally isn't unique to me. This feeling of failure—failure at being a man, failure to be the right kind of man—isn't specific to me either. The pressure to get it right and be a "real man," narrowly defined, has caused me a great deal of distress, anxiety and pain, but I now know it's my special dispensation as a trans man. Most men can't measure up to the unreal expectations placed on them to fit into this identity prison. Trying to live up to the constrictive, constructed social ideal of "masculinity" is a rigged game. No one can be a "real man" in that sense because it's not a real thing! For all the real feelings it stirs up, it's a made-up, fragile concept, so let's blow it up! Embrace your masculinity where you are at right now, and allow yourself the room to grow into the person you want to be! Let's do it together. Let's do it with love.

REASSURANCE ROADMAP

Since this book focuses on self-repair and positive change, I don't want to spend too many pages discussing the "problems" with men. I do, however, want to pass along some potentially eye-opening statistics about what men as a group are experiencing these days. I share this information with you not to shock you, but rather to reassure you that you are not alone in whatever you're going through. Your loneliness is not unique to you. Your inability to connect as deeply as you'd like is not a permanent or incurable state. Men are in pain and most of us suffer in relative silence without an understanding of how to locate or describe our feelings. Even if this information isn't news to you, it's good for all of us to keep in mind why the work we are setting out to do can be life-changing and, in some cases, may even be *life-saving*.

While making your way through this workbook, I implore you to go at your own pace. Don't rush through it. Read the entries in the order that makes sense to you and do the exercises recursively. Consult the glossary of keywords when you need to. Check out the suggested reading materials when you want to pause and put the new concepts you're synthesizing into practical application. Take as long as you need. No one is graduating or getting a certificate of completion. This workbook was designed to effect real transformation in you, the user, through a sustained and integrative undertaking. We will transform together bit by bit, one page at a time.

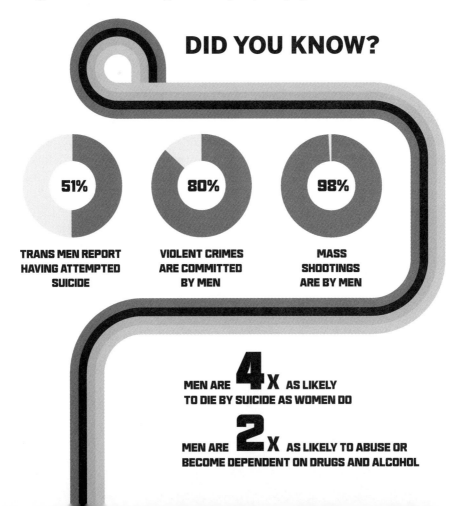

DID YOU KNOW?

51%
TRANS MEN REPORT
HAVING ATTEMPTED
SUICIDE

80%
VIOLENT CRIMES
ARE COMMITTED
BY MEN

98%
MASS
SHOOTINGS
ARE BY MEN

MEN ARE **4**X AS LIKELY
TO DIE BY SUICIDE AS WOMEN DO

MEN ARE **2**X AS LIKELY TO ABUSE OR
BECOME DEPENDENT ON DRUGS AND ALCOHOL

Some major issues men deal with:

· Isolation and competitiveness
· Loneliness and lack of friendship with other men
· Numbness to your own feelings and difficulty in developing intimacy
· Emotional over-dependence on women
· Lack of positive masculine identity
· An unnameable sense of loss due to the absence of fathering
· Cycles of control, depression, frustration and inappropriate expressions of anger
· Challenges in relationship and family life
· Questioning *Who am I?* and *Where am I going with my life?* —especially in relation to midlife transitions

This workbook strives to impart more emotional ease with these and other issues by providing a roadmap to the change you are craving.

Of the items listed above, which ones do you experience on a regular basis?

THE FIVE TENETS

The core philosophy behind Mindful Masculinity is a simple approach to personal growth based on five progressive tenets: awareness, connection, accountability, empathy, solidarity.

Awareness: We start by developing awareness. Awareness of self. Awareness of others. And awareness of the larger systems we are operating in. To gain that foundational awareness, we meditate on some key questions: Who are we? How are we positioned in society? How do we position ourselves? What impact do we have on others?

Connection: The initial act of establishing awareness enables us to make the connection. We begin to understand the systems at play in the world and see how our individual lives touch the lives of others. We start to build communities. We deepen our connections to our authentic selves and to others in our immediate circles and far beyond them.

Accountability: Once awareness has enabled us to make the connection, we need to keep it intact. We do so by holding ourselves accountable. We make sure that, as we flex the new muscles we've grown, we stay aware and open in nonjudgmental curiosity. We learn to prioritize authenticity over the status quo, and self-reflect to see that we're living in alignment with our values. We grasp that getting this growth to stick so that we can experience more means actively maintaining our responsibility to ourselves and others.

Empathy: Having gained awareness, made connection, and maintained accountability, we are now ready to access true and deep empathy. The struggles that other people go through, no matter how divergent from ours, no longer feel so far away. We see others in their complexity and irreducible difference and find commonality in co-feeling. We can now imagine ourselves in others' shoes, treading their distinct paths, while apprehending the greater truth that even in our differences we are all connected.

Solidarity: Once we are able to weave empathy inextricably into the fabric of our being, we will start to stand in solidarity with others. We will come to know that the struggles faced by others are our struggles, too. The pain they feel is our pain. The system holding them down or back is holding us down. This profound recognition opens up the opportunity for you to stand earnestly in solidarity with others.

This may be over your head right now. Or perhaps you can understand it intellectually but can't quite get it at an emotional level. That's okay. Once you've reached the end of this workbook, you will have cultivated awareness, connection, accountability and empathy in yourself. So doing, you will be working in solidarity with other men, women, non-binary people, and all the folks who are fighting alongside you for what is righteous, loving and good.

Try not to skip ahead so you don't miss a step!

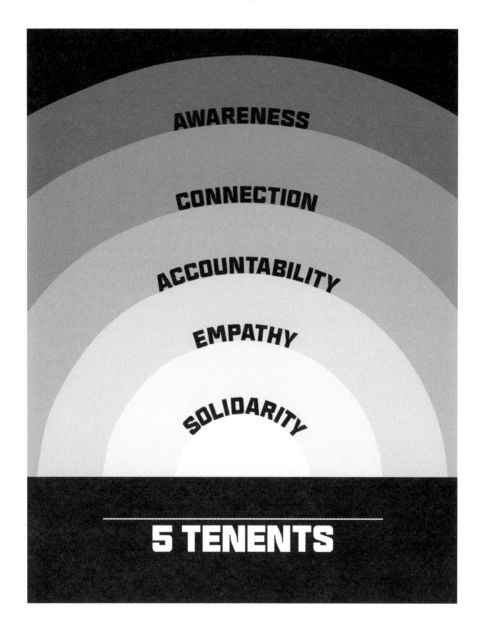

WHAT IS MY GENDER?

A recent psychological study distilled masculinity down to eleven definitive behaviors. To barely paraphrase, here're the greatest hits of normative manliness: winning, emotional control, risk-taking, violence, power over women, dominance, playboy lifestyle, self-reliance, primacy of work, disdain for non-straightness, and pursuit of status[1].

Chances are you could check off some of the items on this list as qualities you currently possess or have possessed in the past. I could, too. And while some of these qualities range from bad news to basic irredeemability, not all are so cut-and-dry or bad-to-the-bone. For instance, I make my work a priority because it is central to who I am and what I hope to contribute in this lifetime, and that's okay. However, if my sense of self-worth becomes totally tethered to my profession, I run the risk of becoming depressed or angry when things with work don't go as planned. This may make me feel out of control and compel me to act out in ways that are unhealthy. So this quality, neutral in itself, needs to be kept in check and remain in balance.

Let's take a look at another one: "reliance on self." A healthy dose of independence is fine and can often serve you, but it can also be taken to an extreme. When I rely too much on myself, I no longer ask for help when I need it. I even smugly anticipate that any efforts made by others on my behalf are guaranteed to be subpar and inferior to what I'd do. I can't imagine that anyone else is capable of doing things up to my standards—a sign that my expectations have become rigid and unreasonable, thus setting everyone in my life up for failure.

We could pick apart each of these list items one by one, noting how even the seemingly helpful ones can hinder us when taken to the extreme in our lives. (Indeed, you may want to do just that and assess the negative and positive roles these tendencies play in your own life.) For now, suffice it to say, all of these behaviors stand to keep us separate from others and force us to fester alone in the alienating aspects of their attributes. But these eleven qualities do not have to be your emotional prison. You do not have to uphold these norms in order to be a man or masculine person. You can be expansively good and whole in your masculinity without having to be great at this narrow list of norms.

Before diving into what makes a good man or healthy masculinity, let's first consider gender — what yours is and how you define it.

I used to travel to colleges and teach workshops about gender identity. We would always begin the workshop with an exercise inviting participants to explore what their gender identity was (identifying it) and how they knew that to be true (feeling it and visualizing it). The exercise is simple and simply intended to bring home the fact that no single defining factor makes a person any particular gender. Let's try the exercise now.

In a moment I'm going to ask you to close your eyes. Once they're closed, I want you to imagine that you don't have a body. Then I want you to clear out all of society's trappings of gender expression and gendered expectations from your mind. By this, I mean try not to associate any activity,

---

1 Mahalik, James R., Benjamin D. Locke, Larry H. Ludlow, Matthew A. Diemer, Ryan PJ Scott, Michael Gottfried, and Gary Freitas. "Development of the Conformity to Masculine Norms Inventory." Psychology of Men & Masculinity 4, no. 1 (2003): 3-25.

any article of clothing, or any specific trait with gender. This will help you escape the trap of too easily identifying gender based on the reductive logic that "men have penises and women have vaginas," or "girls like dolls and boys like trucks." *It's 2020 and you are holding a workbook about mindful masculinity—you know better than that!* Now, with all that out of the way, I want you to take a few minutes to go within. Give yourself at least three minutes, but take as long as you need to really sink into all that I am asking of you. At this point, I want *you* to define your gender. Ask yourself: What gender am I? And, further, ask yourself how you *know* you are *that* gender. Okay, now close your eyes, dive inside yourself, and let's see what you come up with.
(Hint: there is no right answer!)

What is your gender?

How do you know?

I have done this exercise hundreds of times, and each time I find it as difficult as the first. I have heard thousands of people struggle with the ask and the outcome. If we take away physicality and social expectations, what is gender? As a transgender man, I can tell you resolutely that I believe gender is very real. Granting that gender expression is socially constructed, I firmly believe that gender identity is intrinsic to one's self. Gender identity is something we feel and connect with deeply, and have a very hard time defining on our own terms, without making recourse to social expectations and anatomical bodies. I know I am a man because I feel male. What feeling male means to me is going to be different from what it means to you or anyone else. My maleness is not always rooted in masculinity. I celebrate having masculine and feminine qualities, traits and experiences, and I hold space for everything in between. And none of this makes me more or less of a man.

Now that you have identified what your gender is and how you know it is what it is, I'd like you to bring some intention and awareness to your thoughts as you give shape in your mind to the type of man you'd like to be. What follows are some questions designed to open up space for you to visualize how your version of healthy masculinity looks. Please take your time answering these questions.

What does being a man mean to you?

What eleven healthy qualities do you think a man ought to possess?

Do you have or exhibit those qualities?

If so, what qualities do you present resolutely?

If not, which ones do you feel need more attention?

What are three things you can do every day to move towards practicing or exhibiting these qualities?

AM I MAN ENOUGH?

What beliefs do you have about yourself that stand in the way of accepting yourself as a man? (The categories below are meant merely to prompt but not to limit your examples in any way.)

Physical:

Emotional:

Financial:

Spiritual:

Romantic:

Sexual:

Family:

Friends:

Community:

What evidence do you use to support these notions?
(i.e., Men are tall and I am not therefore I am too short to be a man.)

How do these beliefs keep you separate from other men?

In what ways do these beliefs allow you to be less accountable as a man?

In what ways do these beliefs make you feel superior?

In what ways do these beliefs make you feel inferior?

How might you reframe these detrimental beliefs about yourself into neutral qualities or even, in some cases, valuable ones? What if you were to remove the sting from them? Or claim these attributes that you've been using to beat yourself down as things that could hold you up?

Example: If I have spent most of my adult life believing I am not a man, or not man enough, because I cannot pee standing up, then I can positively reframe this fact about myself into an asset. If nothing else, neither I nor my wife will ever have to clean up the mess of urine around our toilet. In that sense, my not standing up to pee is an excellent thing, which doesn't make me less of a man so much as more of a *clean* man. Plus, it's important to note that there are men who do not stand to pee for lots of different reasons, whether by necessity or preference. Standing or sitting at a toilet is not an innate male or female trait, but a learned behavior.

More vulnerable example: The negative "not-man" belief I hold about myself has to do with how I talk about my feelings more often than most men do. I do so because I believe my friendships are made and strengthened most authentically when I connect and commiserate with others over what's going on in my life and how it makes me feel. Whenever I doubt my masculinity on account of my feeling so much and so publicly, I reframe and reclaim my experience positively simply by remembering how much I love being clued into my emotions, feeling them freely and sharing them fearlessly with other men, women and non-binary people. By doing so, I invite others to see me as a someone with whom they can safely share their feelings, as well.

HOW TO BUILD NON-TOXIC MASCULINITY

By Richie Reseda

By the time most of us are twelve, we've punched someone out of pride, lied about sex for Cool Points, and called another boy "gay" for not being "man enough." This is what toxic masculinity teaches us—that we're measured by our physical prowess, how many womxn we "have," and how much money we make.

But what do we do when we're ready to ditch these chains? Here's a quick overview from a guy who puts in a lot of effort—to do it halfway well, some of the time.

When it comes to sex, consent doesn't start in the bedroom—it starts with the first look. Feeling attracted to someone doesn't entitle me to stare, linger, or look them up and down. Contrary to what music videos and middle school taught me, it's not sexy...it's creepy. Just as it's not okay to express sexuality with my body to people who aren't down, it's not okay to express it to them with my face either...

Or with my mouth. Toxic masculinity says that everyone wants to witness my verbal sexual expression at all times, that these are "compliments." But they're not. Rather than assume people want to talk at all, I've found its best to ask for permission and start with regular conversation. "Hi, can I talk to you?" works great. And if they say "no," well, that means "no."

I sometimes struggle with the idea that my manhood, and therefore my value, doesn't originate in my wallet. I drive a '92 Acura Integra that looks like it once decorated a telephone pole. It gets me where I need to go without problems, but I feel embarrassed by it.

The toxic devil on my shoulder tells me I should be in a Model S. That driving a more expensive car would make me bigger, more powerful, more "manly."

To escape the thrall of this mythology, I remember that I'm not valued for what I make but what I give. Driving a sensible car gives me the freedom to financially support friends and family when need be, and to donate to causes I believe in. This reminds me that my purpose is to help, not to ball out.

Getting Man Points for physically dominating others with athleticism or violence is another tough one to shake. It's insidious because I know choosing not to play this domination game can get me hurt, or, at the very least, ridiculed with insults that liken me to "weak" people, like womxn and queer folks.

Combatting this takes courage, dedication, and tolerance for discomfort. When someone "disrespects" me or the people I'm with, I must have the confidence to resist the urge to bark back, get revenge or "come out on top." I instead seek resolution and prioritize safety. This doesn't guarantee I'll be safe, but neither does violence.

Today this is revolutionary—to seek solutions instead of vying for domination. And it's vital. Violence escalates when I fight fire with fire instead of water. Fighting with water doesn't mean allowing myself to be victimized. It means the opposite. The non-toxic way to deal with conflict is to solve problems rather than "prove myself."

This is why toxic masculinity is easy. It means going with the flow and being cool with it when the river cascades off a cliff. Non-toxic masculinity is hard. It means swimming upstream…but swimming upstream sure beats falling off a cliff.

EMOTIONAL TOOLKIT

The emotional toolkit men are given differs dramatically from the kinds non-male-identified people get. Society starts teaching boys (and masculine people) at a young age that they need to be more self-reliant and suck it up when it comes to their feelings. Of course, there are consequences to disconnection and repression for these boys-become-men; if you are encouraged to silence and bury your holistic emotional experience, it can leave you ill-equipped for dealing with your feelings later in life. My own experience serves as an example on this count.

I was about three years into my transition, a young man of twenty-three or four, and about three years into a relationship with a woman almost ten years my senior. We were living together and she was getting sober. I was still a very active pothead, which only stunted my abilities to think or feel clearly more than my gender socialization on its own already did. Thanks to her sobriety, and the attendant skills she was acquiring and implementing in our relationship, I came to realize something big about myself: I didn't even know how to recognize most basic feelings.

I knew all too well about my secondary emotions, like anger and frustration. Anger and frustration are, in actuality, more of a response to an underlying primary feeling; outward expressions of something more formative at the core of a self. But I had no idea how to find out what was underneath them. What core feelings motivated my anger and frustration? How could I even begin to identify the primary emotions at their root? The fear? The sadness? How could I locate the source of my fear? How could I trace the sensations I felt in an immediate, nameable way—anxiety, worry and sadness—back to the more fundamental experiences of loss, disappointment and discouragement I carried at the very heart of me? How could I plumb the depths of myself and become more adept at feeling my feelings?

At the time, my girlfriend was having her own crushing experience learning how to feel and communicate as an adult while having to cohabit with an angsty, raging, figuratively teenaged boy. I wanted to be better. I wanted to understand myself on a deeper level. So I decided to start from a very elementary place and work my way up to my actual emotional age. I got myself one of those feeling charts with the faces on it, the kind designed for little kids, and posted mine on the bathroom wall of our shared apartment. Whenever I would start slipping into an angry or frustrated state, I would hit the bathroom, take a few deep breaths and decipher what primary emotion was underneath. Sometimes I would even gaze at myself in the mirror for a moment to determine which expression on the chart most mirrored my current resting face.

In the beginning, it was really challenging for me to engage my anger differently, noticing it when it flared up and staying with it curiously until it passed. Up until that point in my life, the only feelings I remember having had in my body were anger and frustration ping-ponging back and forth on an exhausting loop. While I'd previously conceptualized the possibility that there were indeed other emotional responses available to me, I'd only really experienced them from the neck up. It was a wholly other thing to allow those formerly abstract concepts in my brain to take perceptible shape inside the rest of my body. Turns out, I'd had a lifetime of grief with unfathomable depths to sort through, and a lack of experience in feeling.

As a man, my desire to complete a task and succeed runs deep. I am most comfortable in action. I think of feelings before I feel them. And I think I can *think* my way out of feelings. But human beings never stop feeling, so there is no winning or finishing up when it comes to emotions. My "manly" impulses needed intense rewiring, major guidance and profound upheaval. Bearing witness to the sadness welled up inside of me, which had made itself known first in hot bursts of rage, wasn't going to be easy or ever definitively over, really, but recognizing and holding space for it and other deeper and more difficult feelings is the only way to open yourself up for true connection to yourself and your world.

Nowadays I approach feeling in a totally different, healthier way, with a daily practice of acknowledgment in manageably bite-sized pieces. My lifetime of grief will always be with me, and while I can process some of it in the present moment, I can't process all of it in every moment. I like to stay in the present, so as not to lose myself in a place of no return: the bogs of murky emotion. Through years of practice, therapy and guided awareness, I have a much broader experience of emotionality. At this point, anger feels like low-hanging fruit to me. It no longer tastes good to go there, whereas it used to be my quick and easy release. Now, I prefer to get to the heart of things, and that requires a practiced awareness and a learned vulnerability from me.

This is a part of the work we will do together. Even if you are a guy that has done this before, let's still do it together. There is never too much self-awareness or too rigorous a practice of emotionality. Am I right?

For the purposes of owning and simply identifying what you're feeling, please resist engaging with "the story" behind the feelings. Let's also resist quantifying feelings. I have found that my own tendency is to put "a little" in front of whatever feeling I express, in order to diminish its mattering and make sure that everyone, including me, knows that it will soon disappear and I don't actually need help. At first, it can be scary saying, "I feel sad," without making that statement as small as possible, so work your way up in scale. For beginners (and anyone else who finds it potentially useful), I have provided a feeling chart of the sort I chipped my teeth on the next page. Please refer back to it as much as you need to.

In this exercise of learning primary feelings, let's also learn to do a body scan and acknowledge our physical experience right now. If you've never done a body scan before, don't worry. I'll walk you through a simplified version of one on the following pages. Somatic experiences are important, too. Our feelings live in our bodies, whether we choose to confront the truth of that or not. So let's choose to start connecting our bodies with our brains and our emotions.

I've scattered check-ins like this throughout the book. When you find yourself at one of these checkpoints, please take a moment to close your eyes, take four deep breaths, open your eyes and then answer the questions that follow. Do not try to fix any of your feelings for now. Just practice bringing awareness to them, acknowledging them, and honoring the fact that you have feelings and are allowed to have them. If you feel so inclined, start to practice this daily. Integrate it into your daily life and see if you too become less reactive and more responsive. It can be amazing how far a bit of self awareness can go.

How do I feel emotionally right now?

How does my body feel?

Is there anything else I notice in my environment?

MOOD CHART

HAPPINESS/JOY: Happiness is a feeling of content and well-being. This emotion can either be achieved through pleasure or the lack of problems in one's life, and can last briefly or for an extended amount of time.

FEAR/ANXIETY: Fear is and emotions that comes from being afraid of a specific object or event, such as spiders or a big test. Anxiety is a generalized feeling of dread or apprehension that cannot be pinpointed to a specific cause, and generally lasts for a long time.

ANGER: Anger is a feeling of frustration that occurs when one cannot reach their goals or feels that something they are experiencing is unfair and unjustified.

SADNESS/GRIEF: Sadness is a feeling of sorrow that is more mild and brief, while grief is a long lasting feeling of sorrow that is normally related to loss.

DISGUST: Disgust is a feeling one gets when they are repelled by a certain object or idea to loss.

MONDAY	TUESDAY	WEDNESDAY	THURSDAY	FRIDAY	SATURDAY	SUNDAY

BODY SCAN INSTRUCTIONS

A body scan is exactly what it sounds like. You scan your body, part by part, to see if anything comes up for you: pain, discomfort, coolness, warmth, tension, tightness, whatever may be. Simply pay attention to the physical feelings and sensations. Don't judge them as good or bad. Don't try to change them. Just become aware of them.

Begin by sitting or lying down in a comfortable position. Close your eyes and take a few deep breaths to calm your mind and body. Focus on your breath. Starting from the bottom with your toes and feet, slowly work your way up your body. Notice if anything comes up as you scan your feet, your ankles, your calves, upper legs, hips, buttocks, pelvic region, stomach, chest, lower back, upper back, fingers and hands, lower arms, upper arms, shoulders, neck, the back of your head, forehead, temples, face, eyes, cheeks, nose, mouth, and jaw. Let your awareness slowly travel back down your body, noticing any other places where there is pain, discomfort or tension. Simply notice this, until your awareness settles back down at your feet.

You don't need to spend more than five minutes on this exercise. Having practiced for years, I sometimes perform this exercise relatively quickly. As you build up your own practice, you'll find it's less a matter of duration and more about being present in your body, locating where felt experiences live in your physical self and listening to what this embodied self-knowledge can tell you.

As in other forms of meditation, thoughts may come up and interrupt your process. Try not to attach to them. Just notice them and let them drift away like clouds in your mind. By coming back into your body and observing your mind with non-attached curiosity, you can form a new, gentle relationship to your brain and your body.

MEDITATION FOR BALANCE BEYOND STRESS AND DUALITY

By Jayson Moton

No matter where you are on the spectrum of masculinity—cisgendered male, trans male or non-binary person of masculine experience—you've more than likely struggled to sync up with gender norms governing appropriate masculine behavior, expression and appearance. Sadly, we often feel this enormous pressure in our families and our communities to be someone we're not, leaving us feeling conflicted and split-off from our authentic selves. It is only when we allow that most pure and vulnerable part of ourselves to express itself freely and fully that we find our greatest strength and come into a true and natural balance within.

I'm a trans man. Twenty years into my transition, and after about forty years of deep reflection, I've come to terms with my own expression of masculinity. For much of my life, I pushed down my emotions, anxieties and fears. I grappled with depression at various stages. But I picked up different tools along the way to help me open up and release some of my deepest challenges, and heal some of the deepest wounds I've faced this lifetime. It's been quite a steep uphill battle, to say the least. However, I am increasingly grateful for this learning curve, as it has led me to a more balanced experience of what it means to hold healthy masculinity within myself. And yes, finding the ultimate peace and harmony is still an ongoing journey.

Over the years, meditation and breathwork have been true life-savers for me, ways to gently let go of my deep-rooted fears, overwhelming inner conflicts and stress. Anytime I sit down for a few minutes and do a breath meditation, I feel as if I've plugged in and recharged the best version of myself. I feel calmer, clearer, more connected and open. It's amazing what a few minutes of sitting still and being present with your breath can do.

The following meditation works on balancing the polarities. It will provide you with meaningful support to connect and bring into alignment the mental, physical and spiritual aspects of your identity and personal growth.

Below you will find detailed instructions and comments on the effects of hand position and breath.

MEDITATION
Come sitting into Easy Pose (cross-legged) or, if a chair is more suitable for you, then sit up nice and tall with your spine straight.

HAND/ARM POSITION:

Raise the arms with the elbows bent until the hands meet at the level of the heart in front of the chest. The forearms make a straight line parallel to the ground. Spread the fingers of both hands. Touch the fingertips and thumb tips of opposite hands together. Create enough pressure to join the first segments of each finger. The thumbs are stretched back and point toward the torso. The palms are separated.

EYES FOCUS:
Fix your eyes at the tip of the nose.

BREATH:
Create the following breathing pattern: Inhale smoothly and very deeply through the nose, filling the belly and lungs. Exhale through the pursed rounded lips in eight 8 equal strokes. There should be a little stop between each of the 8 exhales. On each exhale, pull the Navel Point in sharply. At the end of the eighth exhale, all the breath should be out of the belly and lungs.

TIME:
Continue for 3 minutes. Build the practice slowly to 11 minutes.

TO END:
Inhale deeply, hold for 10-30 seconds, and exhale. Inhale again and shake the hands. Relax.

Comments:
The Five Elements (the Tattvas) are categories that are based in the energetic flow of your life force. If all the elements are strong, in balance, and located in their proper areas of the body, then you can resist stress, trauma, and illness. You also do not get confused in conflicts between the two hemispheres of the brain, as they compete for the right to make and direct decisions. This meditation uses the hand position to pressure the ten points in the fingers that correlate to the zones of the brain in the two hemispheres. The equal pressure causes a kind of communication and coordination between the two sides and the two polarities. The deep inhale gives endurance and calmness. The exhale through the mouth strengthens the parasympathetic nervous system from a control band of reflexes in the ring of the throat. This calms reactions to stress. The strokes of the exhale stimulate the pituitary gland to optimize your clarity, intuition, and decision-making capacities. This meditation resolves many inner conflicts, especially when the conflicts arise from the competition between different levels of your functioning, e.g. spiritual vs. mental vs. physical or survival needs.

Try it for the next week and see if you notice a difference. Try it 40 days or longer if you like it. You can start at 3 minutes a day and work your way up to 11 minutes.

NOTES AFTER PRACTICE

How did you feel?

What did you notice?

How long will you commit to doing this?

RESPONSIBILITY TO OTHERS

By Marquise Vilson

In order to embody what I believe to be healthy masculinity, I must first identify my own toxic behaviors, as uncomfortable as that may be for me. I do this by holding myself accountable for how I show up for others and myself. This is work I must consciously and constantly do. There isn't a magical switch I can flip off to deactivate all the social conditioning that makes me behave in sync with society's expectations of masculinity—it runs too deep. These notions have been passed down to me for generations through my family, my ballroom community, and my Black queer community. To break with this intergenerational legacy, I must actively refuse the privileges available to me simply because they are the special inheritance of men. I must resist becoming a "man's man"—a personal space I have no business dwelling in, nor do I ever want to.

"Man's man," as I read it, is basically code for "oppressive." To me, "man's man" means men performing masculinity for other men, primarily concerned with what other men may think of them as men. Once upon a time, I thought I wanted to be a man's man. But now I am not just a man—and not because of my transness—but because I exist in every way possible. A more expansive way of being and thinking has lead me to healthier expressions—not only of my masculinity—but of all the ways I can and will responsibly show up in the world.

Leaning in and listening more have been my tangible offerings of support to my femme, gender-nonconforming and non-binary trans siblings. Discovering what other people need by listening to the words *they* speak is the only way I can honestly lend myself as an ally. This has required me to intentionally share space with people of various identities, and acknowledge the energy filling up the room with their presence and their voices. Sitting with them and holding space for their triumphs and trauma, seeing them fully and with context: this, they tell me, is what it means to be femme, non-binary, a woman, trans, fat, differently-abled, lesbian, black, poor, Muslim, gay, bisexual… I must acknowledge that they may have been, and may still be, oppressed by men, such that my presence as a masculine person in their midst may remind them of that oppression. I do the work of learning, making an effort to understand and, most importantly, coming to grips with this truth.

I can choose between feeling guilty and shying away from this negative legacy of masculinity that never felt like mine, on the one hand; or I can show up fully and honestly, and thereby help to create real change, on the other. For me, there is no choice here. There is only what feels right, and that is my other inheritance. My self is a blessing given to me by my two spirit transcestors, and no one person better understands my experience than I do. Just as I speak my own truth best, so must I make the space available to all people to speak their truths, especially when that space hasn't been made for them before. I am grateful for my ability to earnestly check in with my masculinity and observe how it is housed, not merely as an honor, but as an obligation and standard I hold myself to. This is the transcestor legacy that lives on in me and I fully embrace it.
ASÈ.

CHECK YOUR PRIVILEGE

Marquise dove right into personal privilege in his piece, unpacking it, stepping away from it, and naming his entry point into becoming a better ally to others. At its core, allyship requires that you as a man or masculine person humbly strive to comprehend the past and present-day hardships and aggressions that others experience—struggles you yourself may never know or never have to deal with in your day-to-day life. So, to make sure everyone's caught up before we get into the next exercise, let's take a moment of mindfulness and bring awareness to what male privilege means in the most practical terms.

On the following page you will find a list of twenty-five examples of male privilege in action. This list is a not-so-subtle nod to Peggy McIntosh's classic, "White Privilege: Unpacking the Invisible Knapsack," assembled in solidarity with the other inventories on privilege in its various manifestations that her piece has since inspired. You may not have noticed or considered many of the following examples of male privilege in your life before encountering them here, and that makes sense. Lack of awareness around micro—and macroaggressions is a privilege in itself, after all. For men of transgender experience or transmasculine-identified people, it's likely you haven't had access to all of these privileges (or maybe you only have after medical transition). As a result, you may have an innate awareness of what it feels like to be on the other side of privilege.

As you read this list, know that it could go on forever. There are more comprehensive lists available online for anyone who wants more examples. The list I've included here is meant to prompt your immediate awareness and usher you into greater understanding and recognition. Do your best calling to mind moments from your life that stand out as examples of this gendered disparity. Be honest with yourself. And do pay mind to the choice Marquise made between feeling guilty and shying away from unpleasant realities or showing up to your truth and helping create change in yourself and your community, as he opted to do. If you have never known another experience outside of privilege, it takes conscious work to be aware of the inequitable status quo that dispossessed folks feel the brunt of every day. Becoming aware of your place in an unjust system is an exercise designed not to make you feel bad, but to help you learn how to be better; how to be healthy despite systemic toxicity; how to be the man you want to be and co-create the just world you want to see.

I've left space at the bottom for you to fill in some manifestations of male privilege that you have seen and recognize in your day-to-day life.

HAVING MALE PRIVILEGE
- You feel safe using gender-specific public restrooms.
- You have a much easier time getting a job and being promoted or recognized for doing a good job.
- You're far less likely to face sexual harassment at work.
- You are not interrupted as frequently as women are.
- You are much less likely to fear walking alone after dark or being in public spaces alone after dark.
- You can see a doctor without fear of your health issues being blamed on your gender.
- You don't fear being sexually harassed, followed or attacked when walking down the street.
- You are paid more for the same job.
- You are seen as powerful and competent.
- You can see people of your own gender widely represented in the media.
- Your ability to make important decisions and your capability in general will never be questioned depending on what time of the month it is.
- If you're careless with your finances, it won't be attributed to your gender.
- If you're careless with your driving, it won't be attributed to your gender.
- You can be aggressive with no fear of being called a "bitch."
- You can be confident that the ordinary language of day-to-day existence will always include your gender. "All men are created equal," mailman, chairman, freshman, he, etc.
- You're not afraid in an elevator when it's just you and another man.
- You're allowed to age with grace and dignity.
- Men in the service industry, like mechanics or contractors, speak to you like an equal.
- No waiter asks someone else what you'd like to eat.
- For the most part, people trust that you can express your wants and needs accurately and do not question you.
- When it's between you and a woman, people defer to you.
- Men don't masturbate to you on the street.
- You don't fear your drink will be drugged at a bar.
- You don't fear getting into a cab or a ride share.
- You have the privilege of being unaware of your male privilege.
-
-
-
-

I encourage you to take this list and integrate it into your daily life. Bring a new mindfulness into the world. Notice how women around you are being treated differently than you are. Be really attentive to women's lack of privilege; its manifestations will run the gamut, from small slights to large inequalities and systemic injustices. Name your privilege, resist it and, if you can, cede your place of power to people who don't have such easy access. Follow Marquise's lead and become a witness and a space-holder.

Men have a tendency to want to name and narrate the experiences of others who are not male, rather than making room to quietly receive information straight from the (non-male) source. Men tend sit unconsciously in privilege and fill a room with their presence. So learn to sit back and listen more. Take note of how often you feel compelled to contribute with your own voice, and start contributing with your open ears, open mind and open heart. Resist the need to narrate! See what comes up for you when you do. Thank other people for sharing and leading. And when you see other men around you taking up a lot of space, try gently inviting them to listen as well. Some really powerful transformation can happen when you listen more than you talk.

FEELINGS CHECK-IN

How do I feel emotionally right now?

How does my body feel?

Is there anything else I notice in my environment?

Take four deep breaths. Inhale through your nose to the slow count of four. Pause. Then exhale through your mouth to the of four.

ON DATING

By Cleo Stiller

They met at a United Nations climate change summit. Rajiv, freshly thirty, had been living like a vagabond, traveling domestically and internationally for work over the last couple of years. He was personally looking to settle down and start a solid relationship with someone. The woman, Sarah, was British but her mother happened to be from the same Indian village as Rajiv's father. Sarah lived in London and was about to move to New Zealand—she also had a nomadic lifestyle. Rajiv took all of these similarities to heart and thought, "Wow, there is real potential here."

But Sarah wasn't so sure. She was sexually inexperienced and just looking for friendship. She said this to him multiple times over the course of the next several months. Rajiv tells me he wrote off her hesitation as inexperience. She asked for friendship; he kept making the moves. He made grand gestures, including a flight to New Zealand and, after enough persuading, moving her from New Zealand to the United States. Surprising no one except him—it didn't last. Shortly after coming to the States, she left him to travel in Central America. He was heartbroken, wondering what he did wrong, when everyone else in his life was like, "Dude, read the signs."

When he found out I was writing a book, and particularly a part on dating, men and women, and #MeToo, Rajiv immediately got in touch. He wanted to explain himself to me and to do so he used a scene from the Disney movie *Cinderella*.

Basically, it's that scene at the end of the ball when the prince and Cinderella share a kiss. Then the clock strikes and she jumps up to leave. He tries to get her to stay, but she's like, "NO! I really gotta go."

All of us in the audience know she's about to turn into a hot mess, so she really, really needs to jet. But he grabs her wrist and tries to keep her there. Then she runs away and he sends henchmen chasing after her to get her back.

"I took away the belief that if I persisted enough, she would realize my love was real," Rajiv says. "What does this teach boys about how far to push, reading nonverbal cues, or whether to accept 'Good-bye!' as enough to stop persisting?"

Dating is awkward. It always has been.

Now take the natural confusion and fear of rejection and toss in the worry that you'll do something to upset someone and be the next #MeToo headline in your friend group. Woof. Intimidating.

Men are spooked! And listen, I hear you.

Let's start at the beginning. The issue underlying Rajiv's story hits at a classic male archetype: men as the pursuer.

"Persistence pays off," says Dominick Quartuccio. Quartuccio used to run a sales team with a $4 billion sales goal in midtown Manhattan, but left the corporate life to be an executive coach. He's now an international speaker, author of the book *Design Your Future*, and cohost of the podcast *Man Amongst Men*. To give you an idea of the kind of circles he runs in, he recently presented a workshop about masculinity at the renowned financial firm Goldman Sachs in New York City. He's learned a lot about men from his clients, who are, he tells me, "high-performing men who are publicly confident but privately confused." The type who thinks, "'Hey, I have everything that I ever worked for. . . . I have everything on paper. Everyone from the outside thinks my life is great, but on the inside I'm feeling restless and stressed.'"

Quartuccio is big into this notion of persistence sculpting how men think of themselves. It's a concept known as "the hero's journey." "As guys, we look at these heroes who against all odds prevail, right?" he says. "However, many times the hero has been told no. Not necessarily in a social or sexual context, but in life, in business, in war, on the sporting fields. If he falls down, he gets back up and keeps going until he gets the prize. He's a relic."

What's one of the most iconic, deeply ingrained prizes at the end of the hero's journey? Boy wins the prize and gets the girl.

Persistence used to make you the hero. Not anymore. And the truth is, it's been on the outs for a while—in fact, a lot of you might have thought we had already left it in the past.

Think back to Rajiv's story. He was following the script he'd downloaded from one of our greatest romance stories: *Cinderella*. Much has been written about the bill of goods sold to women by Disney, but the truth is, we've taught men a fairy tale, too—the fairy tale of noble pursuit. Now I know a lot of you are going to say, "Okay, but Rajiv aside, dogged pursuit mostly still works!" I hear you. I know countless couples who talk glowingly about how the man in the partnership "wore her down." Then they giggle and nuzzle noses. This is real. Persistence often works. However, it's also increasingly viewed as creepy. What are we supposed to do with that?

Let's interrogate whence this concept of persistence as a critical part of masculinity originates.

There's a whole national conversation around an idea called "Man Box culture." Basically, the idea is that we're taught "that men are in charge, which means [that] women are not," Tony Porter says in his TED Talk.

Tony Porter is the CEO of the organization A Call to Men, which provides education all over the world for healthy, respectful manhood. Porter is legit. He's an advisor to the National Football League, National Basketball Association, National Hockey League, Major League Soccer, and Major League Baseball. Basically, he is working with all of our country's top athletes to reshape masculinity. In his TED Talk, he continues explaining what we teach men. "That men lead and [women] should just follow and do what we say. That men are superior [and] women are inferior. That men are strong and women are weak. That women are of less value and the property of men, and objects, particularly sexual objects," he says.

Porter's TED Talk has racked up more than three million views. In it, Porter lays out what he calls "The Man Box." (He got the term from Paul Kivel, who wrote the book *Men's Work: How to Stop the Violence That Tears Our Lives Apart*. Kivel helped develop the term "Act Like a Man Box" with the Oakland Men's Project in the early 1980s.)

Here's a visualization (from https://www.acalltomen.org/). It's a series of qualities men are instructed to embody:

THE MAN BOX:
- Do not cry openly or express emotions (with the exception of anger)
- Do not express weakness or fear
- Demonstrate power and control (especially over women)
- Aggression/Dominance
- Protector
- Do not be "like a woman"
- Heterosexual/Do not be "like a gay man"
- Tough/Athletic/Strength/Courage
- Makes decisions/Does not need help
- Views women as property/objects

This idea of the Man Box has gotten so much play in men's circles that, okay, well, you know Axe body spray? The parent company, Unilever, commissioned a study called "The Man Box: A Study on Being a Young Man in the US, UK, and Mexico."

What did it find?

"Young men reap certain benefits from staying inside the Man Box: it provides them with a sense of belonging, of living up to what is expected of them," it reads. "Friends and parents may praise them. However, when those same norms tell men to be aggressive all the time, to repress emotions, and to fight every time someone threatens them, the Man Box demands that they pretend to be someone they are not, and study results show how violent and lonely the resulting life can be."

How does this relate to dating? Basically, men are still trying to fit into a very specific definition of what it means to "be a man" even if it doesn't feel completely authentic to them, and it's reflected in how they date.

Dating has always been weird and awkward and full of fumbling, and now that generational shifts are calling into question the ideas that underpin relationships between men and women, it feels even more treacherous. As I've said before, men are spooked! The very idea of the masculine roles of pursuing and persistence doesn't hold up as well as it once did. But this is a chance to figure out what your relational needs are and find someone who can help meet them. It can be a relationship built on mutual pursuit.

UNPACKING THE MAN BOX

In the excerpt from her book on *Modern Manhood*, Cleo Stiller refers to a TED Talk by Tony Porter in which he introduces us to the troublesome MAN BOX, an arsenal of all the stereotypical qualities that "real men" in our patriarchal society are expected to possess—anything other or less is less! Let's spend a second unpacking Porter's idea: exploring how we're boxed in by having to behave "manly," how we might expand ourselves beyond these constrictive expectations, and how much more we are as people than any one-size-fits-all-men box can comprehend.

The answers you come up with on your first go may change as you stay longer with the work, so consider revisiting this exercise later on. For now, let's take it one "manly" quality at a time.

The Man Box:
DO NOT CRY OPENLY OR EXPRESS EMOTIONS (WITH THE EXCEPTION OF ANGER)
What comes up for you when you cry or you express emotions openly? What does it feel like?

How could you begin to break patterns around this for yourself? Is there a trusted person in your life with whom you could safely practice greater emotional openness?

DO NOT EXPRESS WEAKNESS OR FEAR
What does weakness mean to you? What makes you feel weak? How does it feel when you are weak or experience fear? What kinds of self-criticism or judgment come up for you when you do?

How can you reframe weakness or vulnerability as less fearsome, even positive qualities? How might it feel to allow yourself the vulnerability of expressing fear to another person?

In what practical ways can you open yourself to expressions of fear or weakness?

DEMONSTRATE POWER AND CONTROL (ESPECIALLY OVER WOMEN)
What are some ways you exert power and attempt to control in your life?

Of these, which tactics are useful and which are harmful to yourself and others?

In what ways has your desire for power and control created problems in your relationships?

What feelings do you notice motivating your will to power and control? How might you attend to those feelings directly and nurture yourself in those potentially tender places?

What would it feel like to let go of some aspects of control?

AGGRESSION/DOMINANCE

In what ways has the will to aggression or dominance caused you or others harm in your life?

What can you do to be less aggressive and domineering?

What alternative ways could you respond whenever you feel inclined to dominance or aggression

PROTECTOR

What aspects of being a "protector" feel good to you? In what life situations have you found this identity helpful?

Has the expectation of being a "protector" ever felt limiting to your sense of self?

Has playing the role of "protector" ever disrespected, harmfully disrupted or diminished other people in your life?

What would it feel like to share a sense of obligation or responsibility with others? What would it feel like to want protection or to be protected by someone else?

DO NOT BE "LIKE A WOMAN" AND DO NOT BE "LIKE A GAY MAN"

Do you fear that your desires, impulses or tendencies aren't "butch" or "manly" but actually "femme," "feminine" or "gay"? Name some of these qualities here and honestly conjure up any negative associations that come up.

Do you believe that "femininity" or "gayness" are inherently bad, inferior, or problematic? If so, what makes them negative or undesirable in your mind? What concerns do you have about being associated with them? What feelings or fears do you think might be motivating that value judgment?

How can you reframe and reclaim these aspects, tendencies or behaviors as positive and integral aspects of your whole being, such that they become masculine or male simply by virtue of association?

Can you tie any of these conventionally "unmanly" qualities to "real men" you admire? Name-check a few of them here.

TOUGH/ATHLETIC/STRENGTH/COURAGE

Do any of these attributes stand in the way of your understanding or measuring up to what makes you a man or "man enough"? If so, which ones and why?

Do you believe that these traits are specifically male or masculine?

In what ways are women and others also athletic, strong, tough and courageous?

MAKES DECISIONS – DOES NOT NEED HELP

How has the pressure of "not needing help" negatively impacted your relationships? Has it ever caused you pain? Has it harmed others in your life?

What would it feel like to ask for help? Whom do you feel safe asking? What would you like help doing? How would being helped help you?

VIEWS WOMEN AS PROPERTY/OBJECTS

In what ways have you viewed women as objects? Try to call a specific moment to mind.

Have you ever felt that you were owed something by a woman? If so, when? What for? And how did you act as a result?

Taking honest stock of your past, consider if you've ever devalued a woman or treated women as "less than" in your life. Bring to mind undeniable, big instances along with less obvious examples of this behavior.

What do you think was blocking you from seeing women as equal to you or equal to men? Do you feel any fear behind your sense of their inferiority? If so, what are you afraid of?

EMOTIONAL REPS: STRENGTHEN YOUR EMOTIONAL CAPACITY

By Mike Sagun

Masculinity has gone viral. And there are as many different perspectives on the subject as there are people out there sharing their thoughts about how masculinity has impacted the world.

Personally, I don't think the problem is with masculinity itself—and it certainly isn't a gender-specific issue—but with the way today's media has directed the discussion solely towards men.

The dissonance I see in that scenario (and maybe the confusion I feel about it) arises mainly from a shift I've witnessed in the "culture of manhood" and the prevailing ideas about what it means to be a man today. Masculinity isn't toxic. Femininity isn't toxic. To my mind, the trouble arises when we conflate masculinity and femininity with gender as such, when we're actually speaking about energies. If you're reading this, you probably already know that, no matter how you identify, you have both masculine and feminine energies. We need a balance of both to live at our fullest capacity. You can also probably recognize the behaviors and expressions of toxic masculinity, i.e. violence, phobia, and bullying, most commonly, none of which are specific to men. But numbers and data don't lie. Most violent crimes, murders, mass shootings, and suicides are committed by men.

Period.

Bottom line: men need help. At The Unshakable Man, my men's coaching practice, we help men take emotional reps. Just as a personal trainer helps people strengthen their bodies, so we help men strengthen their emotional capacity.

What does that look like?

If we want to heal toxic behaviors in other people, it starts with some deep introspection within ourselves, then some awareness, and, finally, a bold new action. When we've done our work, we can help others.

Now this might be uncomfortable for you, and that's okay. The discomfort means you might be stepping into the uncharted territories of your heart. The discomfort also means this is an opportunity for you to grow.

Take a few deep belly breaths. Relax your face and jaw. Drop your shoulders. And let your gut stick out. Don't worry, you don't need to impress anyone right now.

We're going to travel back in time.

Take yourself back to a moment in your life when you hurt someone. Maybe it was something you said or did that caused deep pain. Maybe you reacted with violence or aggression. Or maybe you ran away and isolated yourself. And maybe it ruined your relationship.

Bring to mind what was happening and who was there. Notice the circumstance. And bring to your awareness the emotions *you* were feeling.

Anger is probably the first emotion that came up for you. But what might be underneath that? Anger is usually a secondary emotion, beneath which there may be embarrassment, rejection, sadness, defensiveness, or shame. Notice what specifically brought up that reaction for you.

Be honest with yourself here. What triggered you to inflict pain on another person?

What were you protecting? — Your pride? Your reputation? Your idea of what it means to be a man?

What were you scared to lose? — Your sense of self? Your sense of belonging? Your identity?

What were you projecting? — Domination? Overconfidence? Scarcity?

Take a deep breath. And put that memory to the side.

Now bring yourself back to your childhood. Find a moment in your childhood when an older figure reacted similarly to the way you reacted in the previous memory. The pain that was being inflicted didn't have to be directed at you, it could have been directed at someone else.

Perhaps you saw an adult do or say something that caused pain.

Perhaps you saw an adult react in violence or aggression.

Perhaps you saw an adult run away and self-isolate.

Reflecting back on that first memory, how much of this reaction was learned from a parent, family member, caretaker, teacher, sibling, or even the media?

This might be difficult to own, so take a moment to reflect back on the different times in your life when you reacted similarly to that adult figure.

Take a deep breath. And let it all go. You just practiced an emotional rep. Nice work.

My point: Your harmful reactions in the past were most likely learned. These are patterns that have been strengthened over time, growing stronger each time you reacted that way. This may be tough to sit with, but you can only change by becoming aware of your reactions. In these intense situations, your nervous system gets activated, which shoots you into survival mode.

In survival mode, three things can happen — we fight, run away, or freeze.

Some studies suggest our nervous system isn't just ours, but the nervous system of our parents, grandparents, and great-grandparents. We weren't responsible for learning our toxic behaviors—neither were the generations that came before us. But it is our responsibility to unlearn these toxic behaviors and break these patterns.

The good news is that we have brains that can shift and learn new ways of responding. It's simple in theory, but much harder in practice.

The next time a destructive reaction pops up, catch yourself before you react, take a few deep breaths, and slow your nervous system down. Slowing your body and nervous system down will help you think constructively. And you won't be primed to inflict any pain.

Even catching yourself mid-tirade will help you retrain the neural pathways in your brain to break that pattern of hurt.

This exercise helps us develop a connection with ourselves. It helps us forgive our flaws and allows us to notice where we can improve. And it helps us become aware of the changes we want to make in ourselves so that our reactions don't hurt other people.

This is emotional awareness. This is ownership of our past hurts and traumas. This is healthy masculinity.

RECOGNIZING EMOTIONAL TRIGGERS

Let's take a moment to write about this exercise that Mike Sagun led us through.
Take yourself back to a recent moment of conflict in your life when you hurt someone. Bring to mind what was happening and who was there. Notice the circumstances. Bring to your awareness the emotions *you* were feeling. Describe this moment and your feelings in as much detail as you can remember:

Be honest with yourself. What triggered you to inflict pain on another person?

What were you protecting? — Your pride? Your reputation? Your idea of what it means to be a man?

What were you scared to lose? — Your sense of self? Your sense of belonging? Your identity?

What were you projecting? — Domination? Overconfidence? Scarcity?

How could you have handled this situation differently?

You can always return to this type of inventory to gain a better understanding of your reactivity.

INTERVIEW WITH ASHLEE MARIE PRESTON

This following is an excerpt from a longer interview conducted with Ashlee Marie Preston by Rocco Kayiatos for *The Intentional Man* podcast.

Rocco Kayiatos: What do you think makes a good man?

Ashlee Marie Preston: Empathy is a top one for me. I think there's strength in vulnerability. I know that, [when I was] growing up, images of masculinity that I saw were men who were emotionally unavailable or they didn't show these certain traits, like love or joy or laughter. They had to be stoic, in a sense. It takes more strength and courage to allow yourself to become vulnerable than it does to completely close yourself off. And that's not only in relation to women, but even in relationships in brotherhood with other men.

A conversation that I have been having more recently is about men who date trans women: what that could look like if they had other men in their lives who were more supportive of the fact that they were happy instead of trying to add their own fear and projecting their own insecurities onto them, which makes the other person insecure. And then there's just this echo chamber of insecurity and fear. That's always coming from this idea or fear that they'll never have enough or be enough.

So the mantra, or the idea, that I would always ask is: What makes me enough? It sounds very simple, very basic, but even as a woman—I think it's universal so if you're someone of non-binary experience, same thing—*What makes me enough?*

Is it how society perceives me and how I perform or show up? Is it the pieces of myself spiritually that I allow other people to access? Is it my creativity? Is it my voice? I think that what makes a solid man is someone who can build up that identity without having to hold onto the constructs of gender presentation.

RK: It's really beautiful to think about [how] the starting place for men to become better allies to women is actually [men becoming] better allies to themselves and to each other.

AMP: Well, we can't transmit something we haven't got. If I don't respect myself, if I'm not considerate of myself, if I'm not compassionate, loving, kind, forgiving of myself, how am I going to transfer that to another human being?

So the best way to be an ally to [women] is to hold space for us, and that can look different across the spectrum. It could be holding space for us in the boardroom, at your job, at executive levels. Holding space for us could look like allowing us to have our experiences, our own thoughts, our own aspirations and goals, without feeling this intrinsic need to shift it or to influence or to guide it. Or, as social media culture calls it, mansplaining.

I think holding space for us could look like not expecting us to do all of the labor ourselves of advocating for women, whether it's trans women's rights or reproductive rights—which isn't just [about] women, it's also across the spectrum—or whether it is [advocating against] rape culture. Another way to hold space is to just be mindful that full agency is not just about decision-making, but it's also how we honor our presence in specific spaces.

The other thing is to support us economically. We already know that there is a huge pay gap disparity—socioeconomic disparity—among women versus men. When there is an opportunity to support the work, the labor, the creativity, the vision of women, the best way to be an ally is to show up for that. It's being willing to give up some of your space.

More specifically, it's just important to exercise empathy. In terms of doing the emotional labor, I think it's up to men to come up with what needs to happen, so that we don't live in a country where our president can grab women by the genitals.

WHAT MAKES YOU ENOUGH?

Ideally, reading the interview with Ashlee Marie Preston has you already contemplating the question she posed to readers: What makes me enough? Think about ways in which you have felt deficient and how that feeling has impacted your ability to show up for others as the most supportive version of yourself. What were your initial thoughts or reactions to her remark, we can't transmit something we haven't got? I encourage you to reflect on all of this here.

What are some ways that you don't respect yourself?

In what ways do you not show consideration, compassion, love, kindness, or forgiveness to yourself?

What makes you enough?

With what feelings or values do you want to align yourself and transmit to others?

FEELINGS CHECK-IN

How do I feel emotionally right now?

How does my body feel?

Is there anything else I notice in my environment?

Take four deep breaths. Inhale through your nose to the slow count of four. Pause. Then exhale through your mouth to the of four.

MY DISABLED MASCULINITY

By Andrew Gurza

Whenever I think about masculinity, a particular image always comes to my mind: a strong, powerful, muscular, beautiful able-bodied man. In other words, the essence of what makes a man and the archetype I have definitely sought out in potential partnerships with other queer men. All of this is painfully funny, given that you wouldn't see any of those key markers of masculinity if you were to look at my body. First off, I am not at all able-bodied; I use a power wheelchair to get around. And second, I'm not beautiful by conventional standards (at least in my own estimation), in part due to the ways in which my disability has affected my body: my legs atrophied, my hands deformed, and my belly cookies and crippledness in equal measure. So you can see, there's really no way I resemble that picture of perfect masculinity we all know so well (some of us biblically).

It's not just the normative dating world that throws my manhood into question. I feel like my masculinity gets sized up and doesn't measure up in disability communities, too, where the same muscle-man fantasy abides. The disability community gets bombarded with images of hyper-masculine men gliding across the floor in their sleek manual chairs as they work out at the gym or kill it on the basketball court. These men are examples of perfectly acceptable disabled people; they look beautiful enough to pass as "normal." Picture these perfect men in their perfect chairs and then see me: I roll into the gym on my three hundred-pound powerchair, my belly and my big smile, and no one knows what to do with me, neither able-bodied people nor people with disabilities. I am not really a man to either of them. Instead I'm this alien figure they have to learn how to be around. And that's been really hard for me, if I'm being honest.

But all that being said, and no matter what others have said, I know well enough for everybody that I am a man. There's a place for my masculinity in my disabled body. Sure, it doesn't conform to narrow, antiquated ideas of "what a man ought to be," nor does it match up with the new gay masculinity that prioritizes sex appeal over substance. My masculinity is unique to me—it's mine specifically—and it is not confined by arbitrary able-bodied standards. Indeed my disability has helped me redefine what it means to be a man.

My disabled masculinity comprises a quiet strength that shows itself in my ability to listen to other people. And I'm a very keen listener: my sensitivity to the sounds of others has been sharpened precisely because I'm disabled person who needs help with just about everything. Which leads me to my next point of distinction. My disabled masculinity is also, most importantly, built on the foundation of being *able to ask* for help when I need it. So much of what we envision masculinity being about is this solo quest where some maverick man goes it alone to find himself, or some trite bullshit like that. Well, my disability makes it damn near impossible for me to do just about anything without the help of someone else, so I have learned that asking for help does not make me less of a man. It makes me a man (and a human), and a well-rounded one, at that.

My disabled masculinity isn't rooted in overcoming my disability at the gym, or passing as a "normal" man so that others will like me. It isn't something to conquer or conceal. I am learning to see my disabled masculinity for what it is and what it does. My disabled masculinity is loving, anchored in kindness and compassion. My disabled masculinity is teaching; sharing the experiences I've had as a disabled man can help other men throughout all communities confront their own ableism, and I want to do that. My disabled masculinity is laughing at the sometimes complicated relationship I have with my body, and letting other men in on the joke. My disabled masculinity is about starting new chapters in the book on how to be a man. And my disabled body has helped me do just that.

ASKING FOR HELP

Andrew Gurza makes the exquisitely simple observation that, "asking for help does not make me less of a man," rather "it makes me a man."

Many factors in my life and upbringing compelled me to become self-reliant to a detrimental degree. Because there was active addiction and some major untreated mental illness in my childhood home, extreme self-reliance became my survival tactic at an early age. The way I coped in childhood was later exacerbated by the unreasonable messaging I received as an adult man; specifically, the expectation that a "real man" doesn't need help. This dangerous combination of childhood coping and gendered social convention conspired to keep me self-isolated in the story I tell myself about how no one can help me. I am alone in my struggles. I've seen this self-sabotaging narrative peek through my life all over the place—in something as benign as staying on top of the household fixes to something as serious as taking care of household finances and something as potentially fatal as managing my mental health on my own. Not only have I stayed in this erstwhile-survival-mechanism-turned-source-of-harm style of thinking, but I have sifted through my past and present for concrete proof of this truth: no one is capable of helping me.

Of course, self-reliance isn't such a bad thing in itself. The result of a lifetime of not asking for help, on the other hand, can lead to unhealthy behavior and everyday expressions of harm or damage to oneself, one's inner circle or community. Relying only on yourself over a lifetime can manifest in a seemingly insurmountable amount of resentment building up inside. Only going it alone can keep us alone, completely cut off from other people.

I'll spend some time looking at the harm extreme self-reliance has caused me in a minute, but I'd like to focus first on some of the incredible gifts and skills I've acquired as a result of nearly four decades spent relying on myself. I am able to handle whatever comes my way. I'm generally undaunted by an overwhelming amount of responsibility. I can tackle most challenges and stay standing and smiling. I know instinctively how to get my way out of or into anything. I can always handle more...

That is, I could until about five years ago, when I realized I couldn't sustain a life on this island of responsibility without cracking. It wasn't the tasks that broke me. It was the cumulative years of exhaustion and resentment around the notion that no one had ever taken care of me. It was backlogged emotions I couldn't name or process, a certain and specific type of darkness, like an amorphous blob clouding my senses and blinding me.

My best friend of twenty-one years had just died a slow and painful death to cancer, and I'd been dutifully by her side, always in action—always doing—but once she passed I didn't know how to just be. I didn't know how to receive the simplest gestures of help or care. I couldn't even let my wife hug me or tenderly put a hand on my back. I had always been operating from a place of "I got this." I'd never landed in such a fragile and vulnerable state of desperate devastation. I felt completely unresourced for the first time in my life.

These last five years have been a painful journey into looking at these harmful behaviors and outdated modes of operating in complete isolation and fear. If I wanted real closeness, if I wanted to put some of the baggage down, I had to learn to accept help. Which meant I had to accept that the help might not be perfect. I had to learn that I didn't have to be perfect. I had to learn how to fail at being a person programmed to DO IT ALL. It's completely unreasonable! And it doesn't make me any less valuable or less capable or less of a man. It's a brutal lesson I am still relearning regularly and in layers. And I'm doing so with gentle, patient love and kindness for myself and others. My hope is that you pursue this work in the same spirit.

Do you know how to ask for help?

Do you ask for help regularly?

When you do ask for help, how does it feel to ask? Do difficult feelings come up when you ask? If so, what are they?

Have you ever felt isolated as a result of not asking for help?

Can you identify times when you need help and don't ask for it? What prevents you from asking for help?

How does it feel to receive help?

Does asking for or receiving help make you feel like less of a man?

Do you judge other men or masculine folks for needing or receiving help?

Do you judge yourself for needing or receiving help?

Do you feel like you need to be perfect in order to be a man or masculine?

What's one way you can practice asking for and receiving help?

What's one way you can be loving and kind to yourself around needing help?

A LETTER TO TEENAGE BOYS FROM SOMEONE WHO USED TO BE ONE

By Jacob Tobia

Young guys often feel that the moment they sprout a whisker, they must grow up on the spot. Our bodies change, and we take that as a signal that we must change our personalities in turn. As a gender nonconforming kid, that's where the fun stopped for me.

When I was a child, I would fearlessly express my femininity; playing dress-up, coloring princesses, and raiding my neighbor's bin of Barbies every chance I could get. I never wanted to become an adult, because I knew that along with adulthood came the expectation that I'd finally learn to get my gender "right," learn to perform masculinity "properly," and learn to "be a man."

So, when my body began to change, I didn't experience excitement. I felt grief. With every inch I grew physically, I grew more fearful of the future. With no blueprints from parents or pop culture to help me figure out what my future was supposed to look like, thinking about life as an adult felt like staring off a cliff.

If you're a teenage guy—even if you're a straight, cisgender teenage guy—I imagine that you can understand what I'm talking about. On at least some level, you're probably having to grow up a little too fast for your liking, and you're likely uncertain about what that means.

As teenagers, uncertainty begets conformity. When we aren't sure what's going on in our lives and we don't know what's happening to our bodies, we try to blend in by mimicking the people around us and the characters we see on TV and online.

For boys, more often than not, those images are of action heroes, soldiers, fighters, and men with hulking muscles. They're of people renowned for physical prowess and athletic ability. They're of people who represent a narrow mold of archetypal masculinity.

In the process of trying to fit into this mold, we are asked to sacrifice quite a lot. We are asked to give up our gentleness, grace, kindness, sensitivity, flamboyance, and enthusiasm; our ability to explore different clothing, fabric, texture, and color; our ability to be publicly emotional, with the exception of showing anger and aggression. Gay or straight or queer, cis or trans or something in between, every male-assigned teenager in our culture is pressured to give these things up. It feels like a mandate.

But what if I, as someone who's been there, told you that you don't have to sacrifice those parts of yourself? What if I, a genderqueer adult who was at one point an insecure teenage guy, told you that you get a chance to determine what adulthood and masculinity look like for you? That you have the ability to be better than and different from generations before?

Here's the thing: every teenage guy in the entire world is insecure, unsure of how to be in the world, just trying to get it right. And when challenged by someone with only a sliver of confidence, insecure people are often easily swayed. This means that the pressures of conformity, although they feel so insurmountable, can be transformed through sheer defiance. In other words: You can change the model of masculinity simply by insisting on defining it for yourself.

As a teenager, I was something of a church-youth-group star. When I first joined as a sixth-grader, there were some pretty strict unspoken rules about masculinity, one of which was: *Girls are allowed to dance enthusiastically when the praise band plays songs, but boys are supposed to be chill and not dance too much.*

I hated that rule. I wanted to shake and shimmy and do all of the motions to all of the songs about Jesus and how great he was. I wanted to throw my hands up in the air and bop side to side and get down with my bad self (for the Lord, of course). But I couldn't, because that wasn't what guys did.

Then a miracle happened. One Sunday night, a high school senior guy who played guitar in the praise band joined the girls at the front of the sanctuary and, by the grace of Goddess, *went for it.* He danced exuberantly, jumping when you were supposed to jump, getting low when you were supposed to get low, throwing his hands in the air like he just didn't care. Because *he didn't care.*

Overnight, the rules changed. All of a sudden, it was cool for guys to dance, to make a show of the whole thing, to be dorky and uncoordinated and expressive and fabulous.

Right then I learned that, as a teenage guy, if you decide you're going to wear whatever you want, regardless of whether or not it's "masculine enough," odds are everyone will go along with it if you're confident.

If you confidently tell your friends that bullying someone else isn't okay, they'll likely stop. If you confidently claim your gentleness and sweetness and femininity, people may actually be impressed. And if you confidently acknowledge that being cruel, tough, or physically imposing has nothing to do with adulthood or manhood, your friends just might get with the program.

With only a touch of confidence, you can build a world that leaves more space for your personhood, kindness, and sensitivity.

Obviously, this isn't equally easy for everyone. If you're the only queer kid or the only person of color or the only culturally different kid in your town, transforming social norms can be more complicated. It can take more energy and finesse, and the stakes might be higher. Remember: You never have to challenge social norms at the expense of caring for yourself or keeping yourself safe.

But here's my challenge to all of you straight, cisgender, socially-secure teenage guys out there: Are you confident enough to acknowledge that your heart needs tenderness? Do you love yourself enough to embrace the fullness of your gender identity—femininity and all? Are you brave enough—scratch that, *empathetic enough*—to challenge the social norms around you?

It took me a while to get it right. It took me a while to find that courage. But today, I walk through life with the same self-assuredness that that guitar player showed in church so many years ago. I define exactly how masculine and feminine I want to be. I choose how I'm going to show the fullness of my gender identity to the world.

DANCING WITH MYSELF

Jacob Tobia's personal story demonstrates the ways in which boys and men are limited in their daily lives, allowed only to enact a very specific set of behaviors that have been deemed socially acceptable and sufficiently masculine in almost all regards. Breaking down that self-limiting mentality and conditioning yourself to act differently is a practice. What resonates with you in Jacob's piece?

Can you recall an instance in your earlier life when you thought your behavior or way of doing something was okay until someone else pointed out it was wrong or gendered? What was that?

How did it feel for you to learn you were no longer allowed to behave in a certain way or participate in a certain activity you enjoyed because social norms or gendered expectations prevented you?

Let's follow Jacob's lead and have a dance party for one. As men, we can feel trapped by our not being allowed to be silly or free in our bodies. Now is your time to push through feeling ridiculous or encumbered by what others think. Make a little playlist or just start with a single song. Pick a time and space where you can be alone and blast the tunes and dance like a kid. Get free with your body! Don't be concerned with looking cool or wondering what people would say if they could see you. Try to let all of that go. Move your body wildly and feel the ecstatic release of dancing. It's not just good for your mind and body, it's good for your soul.

SEX IS NOT A KICK IN THE FACE

By Kirsten King

The first time I found out a boy liked me was right after he kicked me in the face.

While on the monkey bars, Eric swung his body back and forth until he gained enough momentum to reach his foot out and strike me. I let go of the bar as Eric's new Adidas made contact with my face, falling onto the woodchip-filled ground below me. I looked up at Eric, who was grinning down at me, and tried to make sense of what had just happened. Why would Eric kick me? Did Eric hate me? Had I done something wrong? Even then, rather than be upset with him, my first instinct was to search for a justification.

And I got it.

As the playground attendant so gently informed me, Eric must like me. So, naturally he kicked me in the face to show me. I nodded, my eyes still full of tears and my face hot with embarrassment, as she explained the situation. The math didn't add up in my head, but I was used to not under-standing why people moved through the world the way they did; I was little and I thought my only option was to take what adults said at face value, even when it seemed like they were wrong.

As a grown woman, I think about this moment a lot. And most of us have had a moment or a thousand moments just like this either from Eric's perspective or from mine. These moments teach us that being feminine means being polite and bearing it, and being masculine means being strong and getting away with it. We use soft colloquial terms to justify horrific actions: verbal harassment turns into "locker room talk"; sexual assault turns into "playing hard-to-get"; rape turns into "asking for it." And we teach women to carry it all. We bear the burden of cis men's bad behavior on our shoulders daily, and so, preferably, with a smile on our faces.

I wonder if my life would have been different if the playground attendant told me that Eric kicked me in the face—not because he liked me—but because he was an asshole. I wonder whether, if she had told me I deserved better, maybe I would have believed it then, too. Unfortunately, that wasn't something I would learn for myself until my mid-twenties.

Before the first time I had sex, I was warned by my more experienced friends that it was important to fake an orgasm so I wouldn't embarrass my then-boyfriend. As I bled onto his minivan seat (yes, I know), I let out my best pornstar moans, hoping they didn't betray just how much pain I was in.

As I reached my early twenties, dating only got harder. I quickly realized that if a cis man spent money on me, he expected something in return. I made internal compromises in those moments because I was scared, because I didn't want to be impolite, and because telling myself I was making the decision felt better than recognizing I might not have a choice in the matter. I noticed that my discomfort in sexual encounters, whether voiced loudly or politely intimated, usually went conveniently unnoticed.

As a bisexual woman (which for me, means being attracted to people of all genders, including trans and non-binary folks), it was only when I started seriously dating womxn that I felt a shift in the type of sexual encounters I was having. The traditional power dynamics I had known, and the physical fear I sometimes felt, was either not present at all, or present on a much smaller scale. Of course, this is not the case for all queer relationships, in fact, consent in queer relationships is still something we have yet to scrutinize enough. But in my personal experience, dating womxn did teach me more about communication, consent, and personal choice. Here's an abbreviated list of what I've learned thus far:

1. If you feel like your partner is not conscious of your wants, that's a problem.
Whether you're telling them to move a little to the left, or that you're not in the mood, a respectful partner hears you. "It was the heat of the moment" is not an excuse. If you can hear your cell phone ring, or your oven timer beep, then you can notice if your partner is uncomfortable.

2. Though it should be obvious, "no" means "no." Full stop.
In some sexual encounters, my partners hear this word and greet it with the same excitement they would a commencing game of cat and mouse. They think it's dirty talk. It's not. "No," or "no, I don't like that," or "no, stop," or any other version of that should be understood as a universal safe word.

3. Consensual sex can still be kinky sex.
There's a misconception that consensual sex means you can't have spontaneous, or kinky, or passionate sex. That's simply not true. This is why number one on the list is so important. If you're conscious of your partner, you'll notice when they're not into something.

4. You don't owe anyone shit.
I spent too long appeasing people because I thought I owed them something. If someone buys you a movie ticket, or a meal, or a whole damn yacht, you still don't have to have sex with them. If sex work is not your job, then sex should never make you feel like you're exchanging goods for services.

5. You can still be assaulted in a relationship.
Entering a relationship does not mean you're giving your partner blanket consent. They do not own a piece of your body just because you're dating, or in a relationship, or a situation-ship, or a marriage.

6. Consent happens in big and small moments.
Consent does not just mean saying "yes" or "no" to having sex; it could mean being with a partner who doesn't like to be touched in a certain place or a certain way, and respecting that. Never compromise someone else's comfort to satisfy your own desires.

This list is by no means complete, and I'm absolutely not an expert on the matter. I'm simply a person who got kicked in the face and thought about it for the rest of her life, so I started writing about it. Most of us have experienced a thousand moments like the one I had on the monkey bars all those years ago. They happen in restaurants or bars, in bed, in private and in public. But as I wish someone had told me back then: Just because something is a certain way, doesn't mean it should be.

DATING AND RELATING INVENTORY

Taking a look at our own bad behavior in the realm of dating is truly challenging. Just as most of us do not get a "birds-and-bees" talk that actually makes sense, so most of us are never taught how to date or mate in a way that truly respects and honors ourselves and our partners. In fact, most of us have no idea what we even like or what our partners like because sex and relationships are shrouded in so much mystery and inherited shame in our society.

In the next section, Dr. Chris Donaghue discusses sexuality more in depth, providing some prompts to get you more clear about what it is you do like sexually, and how you can enhance your sex life by experimenting mindfully, becoming more aware and respectful of the boundaries and limitations set by both you and your partners.

But before we get there, we need to do some housekeeping. Obviously, not all of us are black-and-white Harvey Weinstein sorts, but many of us may be able to personally relate to the gray-area sexual missteps of Aziz Ansari that went public around the same time. In order to see where you fall on this spectrum of sex and consent, we are going to do a sexual inventory here. It might be really painful to look at your experiences honestly, but it's necessary to shine a light on the dark places if you're ever going to clear them out and make room for better, more mindful behavior in the future.

I know firsthand how painful it can be to look at yourself in this way. A self-avowed feminist, I never imagined the possibility that I myself didn't always respect my partners' boundaries and requests. When I began doing this work a few years ago, I started to think back on each relationship I'd been in and had a revelation: I hadn't respected some of my previous partners' boundaries and, worse yet, I'd justified my bad behavior to myself. In retrospect, I could see a pattern of such behavior emerge across multiple long-term relationships I'd had with women whose libidos were lower than mine. I would become a petulant man-baby throwing a specific type of tantrum whenever we went too long for my liking without sex. I would get mad and start a fight. I would emptily threaten to break up with them. I would belittle them in insidious, diminishing ways. Clearly, I felt entitled to their bodies. Until I read an article in which another man admitted doing the same, I never even realized this about myself. It set me down a path of more personal investigation, mining for these sorts of subtly and more obviously shitty tendencies in my past and present.

Now that I told you what about my past misgivings, it's time for you to own up. I don't expect you to go all the way back to childhood, but let's take a trip back to your first significant relationship. This type of house cleaning is essential to healing. After all, we are only as sick as our secrets.

Partner's name	How did I behave in a disrespectful way?	In the future, how would I behave differently?

ON SEX

By Dr. Chris Donaghue, PhD, LCSW, CST

Cultural norms are so firmly rooted in history, and so deeply ingrained in our individual lives, that many of us cannot imagine letting them go or living outside of them. This is profoundly true of normative masculinity, insofar as it's a cultural touchstone for almost everything in everyday life, binding our behaviors even as it creates oppressive boxes to trap us all. Masculinity is a social construction, and, as such, it socially and psychologically limits our ability to be whole and true selves. The stronghold of masculine norms are felt most powerfully at their intersection with sex and relationships.

As a relationship and sex therapist, I watch many male-identified and masculine people struggle to live authentically and honestly. The cultural idea(l) of "masculinity" informs and reinforces many of the toxic sexual and relational values they express. The policing of these boundaries is rooted in toxic masculinity, homophobia, femmephobia, and misogyny. Our culture is obsessed with the gender binary, of maleness versus femaleness, and we do everything we can to keep everyone locked in one of these two boxes, obedient to the rules defined therein. Escaping your assigned box always gets a person punished. And the people policing this confinement to the binary are not the only oppressors, as everyone participating in the system is ultimately complicit in maintaining it.

Gender expression is an ever-evolving cultural performance, changing in conversation with contemporaneous norms and social values throughout history. And so, as a culture and community, we get to choose what we police as devious, what we oppress and marginalize, and what we deem acceptable or even erotic. Healthy identity, sexuality, and gender presentation are all about creativity and diversity, and, ideally, allow for multiple ways of presenting alongside and outside the masculine-feminine binary. The necessary work before us to buck this system is accepting fluidity. We are all far more sexually diverse than society allows us to realize or explore in our individual lives. What you see as your sexuality or relational style is most likely a watered-down and limited version of your actual, authentic self. In a sexually healthy culture, sexuality would exist in a more open and expansive way, with few to no sexual labels and a greater diversity of experiences available to its members. Labels lead to rules, expectations, and discrimination. Whereas healthy sex is fluid and opens up a multitude of sexual practices, ones that may push people beyond the boundaries of who they thought they were—some of these experiences confusing, others highly arousing, and many lacking a label or name.

Authentic sexuality is buried under a lifetime of sexual development, which is basically the sex-negative bootcamp we're all forced through, working not so much to assist personal development as to shame us and push us into conformity. Very few of us will ever be able to fully overcome socialized homophobia, sex phobia, genital anxiety, and slut-shaming. You are developed away from yourself sexually by your gender, with all its rules and expectations. None of that is about authenticity or pleasure; it is about normalization and limits. Fold homophobia and bisexual or pansexual erasure into the mix; add gym culture and body shame to all this; plus the companion stereotype that masculinity means occupying as much literal space as possible; and thus the policing of your sexuality becomes even more powerful.

You are taught that your body is your project and the site for your self-improvement, and it does seem like the more obvious "fix." It's tempting to stop your work there and focus your self-transformation exclusively into making your body match the "acceptable" male form. But the real work before you is with your body *and* mind. I challenge you to make your mind a project, not just your body. Diet and gym culture have profited off the idea that you need to become something else, something *better*. The really difficult work is learning to radically accept and befriend yourself just as you already are, while trusting and valuing the innate intelligence of your body.

Many myths attached to male and masculine sexuality are problematically accepted, embodied and perpetuated as if they were true. Because these false ideas negatively impact on sexual health and sexual pleasure, healthy sex demands we unlearn these myths and learn to live in opposition to them. I do this liberatory work in the clinical context of my private practice. Most of the stereotypes and expectations by which my clients feel bound are rooted in a gendered logic of power that presumes the necessary sexualness, assertiveness, and top status of *all* men and masculine-identified people. But not all men are even sexual. Indeed, some men experience low sexual desire, and some men prefer emotional connection to sex. Men are also asexual or solosexual (more masturbatory and not desirous of partnered sex). Some men are sexually and relationally passive. Some don't initiate sex and others have a totally receptive sexuality. In a word, one's gender expression or masculine presentation neither promises nor dictates sexuality.

Sexual health boils down to embodying your honest consensual sexual desires. And your sexual truth may very well challenge the gendered expectations and norms that have surrounded you your whole life. Being sexually healthy and having hot orgasms means breaking free from these myths so that you may engage in more authentic sex and feel more authentic sexual desire. Growing out of the socially-imposed limits on male or masculine sexuality is the work that all of us need to do, regardless of our personal gender expressions. It is not always easy, but the payoff is a lifetime of hotter sex, higher levels of arousal, and better embodied connection.

HERE'S THE WORK:

1. Contemplate the ways in which your gender limits you relationally and sexually.

2. Have consensual sex that is outside the expectations of your binary gender.

3. Allow yourself to experience physical attraction to people who aren't your conventional type. Investigate why you are rigidly attracted to a certain type of physicality. When did this begin? Where did you learn it?

4. If you watch porn, watch diverse types of porn and porn that challenges gender norms.

5. Examine how you discuss sex. Is the language you use limiting or oppressive? Do the expectations on you as a masculine person influence the way you discuss sex? If so, how might you change this?

6. Explore how your body and sexuality have felt the impact of cultural oppression in the domains of sexuality and relationality.

BE YOUR OWN IDEAL PARTNER

Now that we have a greater sense of how our past behavior may have been out of sync with the men we wish to be, it's time to start the work of becoming the men we were meant to be. This next exercise is focused on how we want to show up for others in our lives in all our different relationships. Answer the questions below by listing qualities, if you find that form more felicitous for you.

Since our focus has been sex and love, let's first think about romantic relationships. What kind of partner do you want to be? What are the qualities you wish to possess in romantic relationships?

What kind of lover do you want to be? If asked to describe you, what positive qualities do you hope your partner would ascribe to you?

What kind of friend do you want to be?

What kind of brother do you want to be?

What kind of son do you want to be?

What kind of father do you want to be?

What kind of worker do you want to be?

What kind of boss do you want to be?

What are a few actionable steps you could take to become your ideal? Write down some examples of new ways of behaving that could support your desired changes. For example, perhaps you have a short fuse and are quick to react out of anger or frustration and you lash out at your loved ones.

One way you could begin to shift this is through the awareness you created in this exercise and taking some deep breaths before reacting and think to yourself, "is this the type of son I wish to be... is this the type of boyfriend, friend, husband, father I wish to be?"

So if I were to write that down here I would say:
"Be more mindful of my tendency to react out of anger. Take deep breaths before I react."

What are some things you really love and value about yourself in relationships? Make a list of attributes you bring into your relationships:

FEELINGS CHECK-IN

How do I feel emotionally right now?

How does my body feel?

Is there anything else I notice in my environment?

Take four deep breaths. Inhale through your nose to the slow count of four. Pause.
Then exhale through your mouth to the of four.

ON BECOMING A FATHER: MINDFULNESS PRACTICES

By Martin Vitorino, Ph.D.

Growing up, there were things about my dad that I loved. Every now and then, he gave these solid hugs that lasted several seconds longer than hugs usually do and almost suffocated my lanky frame. He said more in his tight grip than he ever could with words. He sometimes patted my head, much like you would a dog, until the static would build on my hair and I had to swat him away. Though he couldn't score a single basket, he took me to play basketball at the YMCA. I remember his willingness to play ball, not because he enjoyed it or was good at it (he was especially NOT good at it), but because I enjoyed it.

I remember I looked up to my dad and admired him, even though he was not consistently warm or present or safe. Sometimes he felt like a stranger who was handed a few kids and asked to watch them while our real dad ran some errands. For the life of him, he could never remember how old my brothers and I were or which grades we happened to be in. Whenever someone asked how old we were, he would often turn to us with a genuine curiosity saying, "I don't know, Six? Eight? How old are you guys now?" Upon hearing us announce that we were actually seven and nine, he responded with an innocent surprise at being so off-base.

My dad led a life of quiet solitude, sequestered most of the time in the basement, obsessively reading the Bible—in paperback and hardcover, in editions with gold-painted pages—from cover to cover, and listening to hundreds of New Testament interpretations on cassette tape. We called this space with its library of born-again Christian texts "Dad's little room." When he wasn't working, he spent most of his time there.

Save for his sprinkling of puns in conversation, he was a pretty serious guy with a low tolerance for silliness. He would often admonish us with an old Portuguese saying. To translate, "the one who laughs is the one who cries." I think about what his childhood must have been like to make him so averse to the laughter and playfulness of his own children, such that he would hit them to stop.

I've spent a lot of time dwelling on moments from my childhood that stand out to me as pivotal because of what my dad did or didn't do. Some of these moments were really kind and tender, and others were significantly traumatic experiences.

I think not just about the impact of these moments, but also the way in which I've internalized his responses to me as an unconscious way I relate to myself. It's as if I keep recreating the dynamic with my father, only internally, with myself. Whenever a need comes up, my inner dad shows up. When I make a mistake, I have to face the internal wrath that is sure to follow. He shows up when I am "too busy" to take care of myself and when I can't seem to find the time to have fun.

My mindfulness practice has shed a lot of light on the ways I treat my heart like a father impatient, often cold and aloof, neglectful and cruel. I inflict much more pain on myself than I experienced in childhood. And it may even hurt more, because it is coming from me. It's been painful to see the way I throw daggers of judgment at my body for not being muscular enough, manly enough, bearded enough, cis enough. I see how simple things—giving myself healthy meals, drinking enough water and having fun–feel like an inconvenience to my inner dad. As I peel back the layers, it is clear that I don't think I deserve basic care, otherwise I'd be giving it to myself.

I think the hardest part about my childhood was the way my little-boy brain viewed all of my dad's actions through the lens of my own value, "how I deserve to be treated," "what I'm worth." I felt like I was a bad kid, like something was wrong with me. I felt fundamentally unlovable. And that core belief still drives the kind of father I am to myself today.

Though there's a long way to go before I free myself from the suffering caused by the belief in my own unworthiness, I have been really helped in the process by a practice I want to share with you now. The practice is rooted in the Insight or Vipassana tradition and adapted from teachings I learned from two of my teachers, Rene Rivera and JD Doyle. The practice is derived from loving kindness, or "Metta" practice, in which one offers friendly wishes to oneself and/or others. The phrases themselves don't have to land a particular way and you don't have to mean them as you're saying them. The very act of saying them is itself an act of self-compassion. Most of the time, these phrases feel like aspirations out of my reach (I am so far from living into them), but I have witnessed a cumulative effect in myself all the same. Over time, I have shed some of the armor around my heart and become a good enough if imperfect dad to myself.

Here are some phrases that have worked well for me:

May I love this body just as it is.
May I love myself exactly as I am.
May I hold myself with tenderness and care.
May I treat myself with respect.
May I pay attention to and be responsive to my needs.
May I care about my pain and suffering.
May I be safe and protected from harm.
May I be as healthy and strong as possible.
May I offer myself a break.
May I be a loving father to myself.
May I be patient with myself.
May I forgive myself for making mistakes.
May I be gentle with myself.
May I give myself permission to be the man I am.
May I allow myself joy, pleasure and fun.
May I receive the care I need.
May I be generous with myself.
May I live with ease and well-being.

If there are times when any of these feel out of reach, I sometimes add, "May I someday be able to…" instead of "May I…" When offering these phrases to myself feels inaccessible, it can help to switch gears and offer these phrases to others, like my brother or my dog or cat. When making these wishes to others by saying, "May you be safe and protected" or "May we receive the care we need." Offering these gestures of goodwill can expand our capacity to be compassionate and caring for those we already love, as well as others with whom we might have more challenging relationships.

What I want to leave you with is this: It just isn't possible to be mindfully masculine and not at the same time be tenderhearted. The two are synonymous. My wish for you and for me and for all of us is that we discover that we absolutely deserve care and that we find the courage to care for ourselves and others.

EXPLORATIONS

What are some of the significant moments that stand out from your childhood involving your father, or maybe his absence from your life? How would you describe the ways you received care from your father or paternal figures in your life?

What paternal qualities have you witnessed from other men throughout your life?

What kind of a father are you to yourself? What are the ways you respond to your needs? How do you speak to yourself? In what ways can you be more responsive to your needs?

How do you show up as a paternal figure to others? How about toward animals, plants, or the environment? In what ways do you nurture others through the work you do either in your profession or through acts of service?

Practice: Imagine a time when you were a child and something painful occured. Now imagine yourself as you are now, visiting this younger version of yourself. What are some of the things your younger self needs to hear from you? What are some loving-kindness phrases from above, or any other adaptations, that would bring some comfort to your younger self? Spend a few moments visualizing your adult self offering compassion to your younger self.

Practice: Set a timer for five minutes. It is important to assume a comfortable position that allows you to be alert but not so cozy as to lull you to sleep. During this time, offer yourself one or more phrases that resonate with what you might need to hear at this moment. You can place a hand on your heart or on your belly, if that helps. Gently repeat the phrase(s) to yourself over and over again. Welcome whatever feelings and sensations arise and simply notice them. Your mind will wander away from the phrases. When you notice that your mind has wandered, gently bring it back to the phrases.

What was that like for you? What did you notice?

*Keep in mind that the effect of this practice is not always noticeable during the practice or immediately following it. The impact may be more of a gradual shift in the way you relate to your own pain and the pain of others. Try it out for some time and see what you notice.

THE DEATH OF PETER PAN

By Trystan Reese

The tattoo machine (I know better than to call it a "gun") seared the thick black lines into my forearm and I wondered what the hell I was thinking. With my low tolerance for pain and a face prone to dramatics, I was exhibiting an embarrassing display of weakness. Tears sprang to my eyes as I bit my lip and tried not to cry out.

"You're doing great," Jesse, my tattoo artist, reassured me. I knew he was lying.

I have a lot of tattoos and during each session, I promise myself I will not get any more. "This one will be the last!" I always proclaim, only to eat my words when a new and beautiful idea comes into my head, and I find myself phoning the shop to make an appointment.

"Why Peter Pan?" Jesse asks me. I smile as I try to formulate my response. Why Peter Pan, indeed.

——

As a child, I never wanted to grow up. Most kids around me held their breath as they waited to be old enough to bike home from school alone, to watch R-rated movies, to drive. I never did. I knew these years of grown-ups feeding me would only last so long, and the years to follow—ones in which I would have to feed myself—would last a lot longer. And when I did imagine being an actual adult, I was committed to living a bachelor's life. I didn't want a car, a spouse, or a mortgage. These things would all constitute "selling out," which I was very much not interested in doing.

It just so happened that I didn't know anyone who had those things and was also like me. As a kid, *like me* meant creative, theatrical, and literate. As a teenager, *like me* meant experimental, liberal, and political. And then, as an adult, *like me* meant transgender. As far as I could tell, transgender people didn't fall in love. They didn't get married. And they certainly never had children. So I decided this was for the best, since I didn't want those things anyway, and I never really gave them any thought.

Until I grew up.

The older I got, the more I began to consider what else there could be for me. By the time I was a teenager and realized I was trans, I hadn't expected to live much past the age of eighteen. There were no trans elders for me to admire. But the years kept coming and I found myself growing into a human being that I very much liked. My youthful spontaneity aged into a mature love of adventure; my theatrical flair honed itself into a profession in storytelling. I joined the LGBTQ movement and met hundreds of queer couples who had gotten married, made a life together, (sometimes) had children together, and were...dare I say it...happy.

Could I, too, be happy?

I was deep in this question when I met the man who would later become my partner. He was a surprise, wholly unanticipated, and we fell hard for each other right away. I had not known what it was like to be loved—actually loved—just as I am. I didn't have to round off any edges for him, didn't have to dull any gleams. He wasn't afraid of me nor was he ashamed of me nor was he in awe of me. He met me on the bridge as a true partner and I was bowled over by it. I started to wonder if it wouldn't be best to grow up for-realsies.

One year into our relationship, my partner's niece and nephew needed a place to stay and so they came to live with us. I soon fell in love with them too, and with our cobbled-together family. These two beautiful children with no place to call home, just as queer people have often had no place to call home, just as, at different times in my life, I hadn't had a place to call home. I loved them. And when I thought back to my childhood dream of growing old alone, free of all emotional ties, I decided it was time to let that go. It was time to say goodbye to Peter Pan.

———

And so I got a black-and-gray tattoo that takes up my entire left arm, an homage to my lost dream of never growing up. I let go of the promise I made to myself never to get tied down by getting entangled with others. I decided that my former life had been lovely—I had learned so much being footloose and fancy-free—but it was time for a new kind of life, a life of bedtimes and sticky kisses and working hard to make the world a good enough place for my children to grow up in. Of allowing myself to be known, and allowing myself to know. Of being seen, in all of my weaknesses and insecurities, and loved just the same. A new kind of living.

And I learned, after all that, that Peter Pan was right when he said: "To live would be an awfully big adventure."

To live has been an awfully big adventure.

I AM NOT MY FATHER

I am no different than any other man, or person, for that matter: I have daddy issues.

My dad was so incredible in some ways and not so much in others. He stayed home with me and my twin sister while my mom worked, so we had lots of time with him when we were little. I idolized my dad. Though he was strong and masculine, he wasn't what you'd call a typical alpha male. He was an *intellectual* one, esteeming education above all else. Financial wealth and career success were less impressive to him than the amount of knowledge someone had accrued. Even as a little kid, I could see that my whip-smart, stay-at-home dad was charming and adaptable. And I loved watching him interact with other parents, especially at PTA meetings, where all the moms would swoon over him. He was a voracious learner and a devoted teacher to me and my sister.

But he could also be cruel, unfair, and irrationally self-righteous. He was condescending, especially to my mother. He taught us that "crying is a manipulation tactic." He yelled too much. He punished us with day-long lectures. He wouldn't take responsibility for the impact he had on his family. (And still doesn't.) But he taught me that it was okay to be different and, when I was, he and my mom continued to love me unconditionally. To this day, he and I wrestle with communicating that love to each other. My relationship with my dad is as much a source of strength as it is a point of pain and disappointment for me. I have to actively work on it on a regular basis. And most of that work is not with him, but about him. I have to choose from moment to moment to forgive him for his painful imperfections as a parent. I hold steady space for the sadness I feel about not having the relationship I wanted with him. I hold space for the forgiveness I can access for him as a man who did his best with the tools he had. I struggle with this every day.

In this exercise, I want you to answer some questions I regularly ask and answer myself.

What are some challenging or problematic qualities your father possessed that you do not want to bring into your relationship with your own masculinity?

What wounds do you carry because of your relationship with your father? Which of his own wounds has he passed on to you?

Do these wounds impact the way you relate to yourself as a man or the way you relate to other men?

What would you say to soothe the little-kid part of you that didn't get the fathering you needed?

What would it take for you to see your father as an imperfect man who did his best and forgive him?

What are some qualities your father possessed that you admire?

In what ways did your father's masculinity influence or inform how you approach your own masculinity?

In what ways do you feel you connect well with your father?

If you are a father or wish to be a parent someday, what kind of father/parent do you want to be? What traits are vital to your version of healthy fatherhood/parenting? How would you nurture your child in the way your inner child needs nurturing it may not have gotten? How would you like your child to feel loved and seen?

BLENDED LEARNING

By Jamison Green, PhD

People who have never experienced the sort of dissonance I felt separating my gender and my sex—features most people feel are so integral to who they are as to be interchangeable concepts—may never understand that what I and people like me experience is actually a very real phenomenon. Some people have to change their sex in order to achieve the experience of ordinary life; some people have to change their gender. For me, my gender has always been masculine, male, and until I was firmly ensconced within a body that was also perceived as male, I was not able to experience wholeness in my being. Some extreme anti-essentialist feminists long ago proposed that gender is a social construction; they staked their claim on gender equality by arguing that there was no real difference between women and men. I disagree. There *are* differences: hormones induce distinctions and activate receptors in the body that cause changes in body fat, bones, muscle, sinews, hair, pores, glands, thought processes. But that doesn't mean that these changes are reductive or that it's necessary or appropriate to apply a value judgment to them. There are personality differences, and sometimes those features that support personality distinctions are presumed to be essential, archetypal, stereotypical; this is the counterargument of gender essentialists. Neither of these extreme inclinations toward social constructionism or essentialism are helpful to anyone!

I believe men should become conscious and cognizant supporters of feminism because the blend of male and female perspective that is possible is so much more rewarding, more productive, more constructive than the traditional, isolated masculinist point of view. But I was lucky: I was born "in-between," so uniting what others thought of as "polar opposites" came easily to me. I don't think men and women are necessarily that far apart, but the ability to recognize and appreciate the differences without becoming resentful of—or pandering to—what turn out to be the real social constructs, the arbitrary limitations or constraints that cultural beliefs impose upon both women and men—can be surprisingly difficult for some people.

Learning to let go of the moorings that tether us to limiting concepts is an exercise in fearlessness, in weightlessness, in experiencing a fullness of being human that may be surprising. Not everyone can do it. At least, not yet... As we break down the barriers between those things that men and women do, we can also change our ideas about what—and who—men and women are. And we can then also acknowledge all the many ways that people can be and are already in-between the sexes, the genders, and/or the sexualities, all of which are so much more than binary. We all have our own unique place to occupy within the full spectrum of humanity.

Learning to let go of the expectations of others, of our fears that we are not measuring up in some way, and learning to find our own center and be fully responsible for ourselves, our beliefs, our actions, and the choices we make in relation to others, to me that is the essence of being an adult. When people struggle with their masculinity or their femininity, or rely on their gender to exert power over others, that struggle or that exercise of power seems to me to reflect an inability to be responsible for oneself and a lack of moral compass to guide one's behavior. I don't care what kind of body is using gender or its absence in whatever abusive way: Abusive behavior is wrong, it is unhealthy, it is phenomenally sad and damaging to others and to the self.

People judge each other based on how we look and how we behave. Men with a sense of feminist consciousness or social justice values are invisible. We don't get credit for what can't be seen. My father died before I transitioned, but I believe my father saw me. I believe he valued my uniqueness, and my autonomy. He encouraged me to live fully, to be honest, to care about other people. My father would not have called himself a feminist, but he had integrity, and he modeled kindness and logic, skill in the kitchen and skill with woodworking tools, the ability to laugh at himself, and the conscientiousness to always clean up after himself.

My mother said to me once when I was probably ten or twelve years old, "Your father never leaves his towel on the floor or his dirty clothing all around; he picks up after himself, and that's a wonderful thing."

And I thought, "So this is a stellar quality in a man?" But what I said was, "Is that unusual?" She said, "Yes, I think it is."

"That's pretty sad," I said.

"But your father is a very good man," she told me. And she was right.

Picking up after himself was the tip of the iceberg. Underneath that surface, he offered us strength, love, skills to share, and respect for self and others. That's the kind of man I can choose to be.

INTERVIEW WITH WADE DAVIS

The following is an excerpt from a longer interview conducted with Wade Davis by Rocco Kayiatos for *The Intentional Man* podcast.

Wade Davis: After doing the work of reading and learning about feminism, I no longer use the term "ally" because I learned that anytime you have an oppression that exists—whether it's racism, sexism, ageism or what have you—all of those issues at some point intersect.

Any form of oppression is never going to be localized. It doesn't stay local. It goes; local, regional, global and so on. When you learn that sexism does create less spaces for men to show up in various ways, you realize that you can't be an ally by trying to rid yourself of patriarchal practices or sexism. I am actually a solidarity partner. Because we are actually doing the same work to benefit each other. Now the benefit may look different, but as a man I am still benefiting from it. Therefore, I am not really their ally. Our futures are tied, so we are doing this work actively in solidarity with each other.

When you frame it like that, you can push men to see it as something that is beneficial for them; it becomes personal. It moves away from the intellectual and it moves into the personal. Then, people will take different risks. If I have a child and this child requires certain medical services, I am willing to run through a brick wall to get this child those services. But if it's someone else's child, I may not take those same risks because it's not as personal.

How do we make those connections personal? It's by making sure that people see this work, or see oppression as connected. I hope men can do the work to see that is true. That if femininity is policed, then masculinity is policed. That if there is only one way to show up in the world as a man, then what happens to you when you don't show up in that exact way? Now you are outside of the realm of safety. I would hope that men can understand that when we are talking about masculinity, we are actually talking about masculinities, with an "s" and if there's a spectrum or numerous ways that people can show up as masculine, then it can't be finite. It has to be infinite. It has to be open and spacious. Because if it isn't, as James Baldwin said, "They come for you in the morning and they are coming for me at night." So, I try to really expand the notion of masculinity.

RK: I watched a speech you gave at Tech Open Air conference in 2019 where you mentioned that, at Netflix, you are moving away from diversity and moving towards inclusion. Can you speak more on that distinction and why it's important, especially in a workplace?

WD: All of us are diverse, even white men who are at the top of the food chain. They are not all the same. What I try to do is encourage people to focus on this idea of representation. To say, "Alright, if we want to be more diverse, can we move one level down? Are we thinking about multiple identities and seeing which of these identities are not represented in the room?" Inclusion gets to a space where we start talking about power and, when you start talking about power, we have to consider that though, yes, there may be a woman in the room, there may be someone that identifies as LGBTQ, there may be a white man in the room and there may be XYZ in the room, but if you are feeling included, there has to be shared power. Or, at least, a genuine attempt for there to be shared power. Can we wrestle with ideas of power when it comes to decision making, when it comes to who gets to speak the most, or who gets to tell their stories? Inclusion is the space where we have to talk about dynamics of power. Whereas diversity is really mostly about visible markers of identity, that are important, but just because we have diversity in the room doesn't mean that those folks are represented and that they have a level of power.

RK: How can men in positions of power in a workplace work in solidarity with women?

WD: We have to humble ourselves to realize we don't know it all. That's a starting point. To say, "Okay, I don't know everything and I am going to be open to listening and learning. I will push myself to not have judgment around everything that I am being taught. I am going to think about it and interrogate it, but I am not going to judge it because it makes me feel a certain level of discomfort."

Once you get to a space of listening, learning and resting in the discomfort, then try to think about what is making you uncomfortable. What is at the core and root of making me feel this discomfort? Oftentimes it is the status quo that has benefited me is shifting. All of the things I get to take for granted, by virtue of identifying as a man and the world seeing me as a man, all of those benefits are shifting and moving and that makes me feel a certain level of discomfort. So when you feel that discomfort, you have to name it! [At] that moment, tell someone, "XY and Z is happening and I am feeling a lot of discomfort. Here is what I am feeling uncomfortable about…" And hopefully when they name that discomfort, they realize they're still here and nothing bad is really happening. The fear they are having is valid, but they didn't die. I think for a lot of people it's the discomfort to name something like, "When there are more women in positions of power, that means there is less space for men." And that is actually true. But then think about, "What makes me think that only men deserve to be in positions of power? Where did I learn that?" It goes back to reflexivity, interrogation of all of my fears, naming those fears out loud, then reading more and learning. It really becomes a cycle of learning, reading, admitting, owning and doing it over and over again, until you get comfortable doing it. And you realize by doing it continually, you are growing at such an amazing rate. And you start to realize that your life can get infinitely better and you don't lose anything, you gain more. And it becomes easier to love yourself.

MARKERS OF PROGRESS

What are your key takeaways after completing this workbook?

Have your thoughts on masculinity changed?

What concrete shifts have you noticed happening in yourself since beginning this workbook?

What are some changes your community or intimate circle have noticed?

How will you continue to stay engaged in this type of work?

What are three goals you can set for yourself in continuing to do this work over the next few months?

Do you have friends that could benefit from engaging in this same work? How can you introduce it into their lives in a gentle and encouraging way?

CONCLUSION

Now that you have made it to the end of this workbook, you may be wondering what's next. What is the solution to all of these problems with masculinity? If I had to distill it down to one word, I'd have to say: empathy. Of course, this means empathy for others, but it also means allowing there to be compassion for men and for yourself as a man. Stepping further into your integrity means exemplifying this compassion, which requires patience and a commitment to change. It means unlearning and dismantling the social programming that limits you. It means learning and continuing to commit to a lifetime of learning. It means persistence and perseverance in the face of a culture that is not rooting you on in your efforts to do better. It means taking all of this on while standing resolutely in a place of love. It means acknowledging all the pain you have caused others and yourself, forgiving yourself for it, and practicing doing better in every moment.

Finishing this workbook by no means means your work is done. It's an ongoing practice and a pledge to yourself you choose to renew daily. Approach this type of work by taking it one day at a time. It's not enough to show up to the Women's March with a sign that demands your recognition as an ally. You have to show up every day and do this work in every space. Integrate what you have learned and unlearned recursively into the fabric of your being. Move forward by transmitting all of this to others and do so in a way that is neither braggadocious nor disruptive, but rather humble and mindful.

Let's show up in our lives as men capable of being good listeners, constantly and continually available to learn and make room. Let's recognize and name privilege and misogyny when we see it. Let's advocate for women and non-binary folks in our actions, by lifting our voices and lending our ears. Let's begin to overcome the patriarchal ideals of masculinity we witness in our own behavior and let's refuse to participate in this broken patriarchal system. Let's reject the rigid standards of gender that have been trapping us all and apply the compassion and patience we have discovered in doing this work. Let's help other men in our lives understand how they might also do the work right now.

My hope for you, dear reader, is that, in completing this workbook, you have transformed some of your thoughts around feminism, allyship and your participation in the patriarchy. My hope is that you have dropped some of your defenses and let go of your need to be seen as a "good man," becoming instead a man that can see the good work that needs to be done and how you can help do it. My hope is that you have gained a deeper understanding of gender and the inequalities experienced by others, and that this has deepened your desire to be a part of the solution.

While we allow ourselves the space to experience growing pains, let's remain open to hearing about how we can make more space for those around us to grow. As we integrate all of the discoveries we've made about ourselves into the way we carry ourselves in this shared world, let's remember that the act of listening and the art of letting go of being right can elicit the most powerful results and make the most profound change.

At the end of this book, you will find a list of suggested reading and viewing materials that can further expand your understanding of gender, feminism and healthy masculinity. I implore you to continue your education and extend your quest for healing and self-improvement. If you crave community and dialogue, try attending a men's group in your area, invite a friend to do this workbook with you, join The Intentional Man Project and find an online community ready to do this workbook together, go on a retreat, start your own men's group! Stay engaged and remember: This work never ends. And that's a good thing.

ABOUT THE CONTRIBUTORS

Wade Davis
Former NFL Player Wade Davis is an educator and advisor on gender, race, and orientation equality, and currently the VP of Inclusion for Product at Netflix. Wade was the NFL's first LGBT inclusion consultant, where he worked at the intersection of sexism, racism, and homophobia to build inclusive leadership strategies and engagement initiatives. Prior to joining Netflix, Wade consulted for Google, P&G, Viacom, and Bacardi. Wade is a new board member of the Ms. Foundation for Women, as well as a United Nations Women Global Impact Champion, a founding member of VICE's Diversity and Inclusion Advisory Board with Gloria Steinem, Roberta Kaplan and others. Wade is also on the boards of Sparks + Honey and the MAD Foundation, Chef Rene Redzepi's global food sustainability initiative focused on the future of food. Recently, Wade was named a Global Champion for Girl Up, a program of the United Nations Foundation. In 2018 Wade built a "Men's Gender Equality Development" leadership program that launched with the United Nations. He is currently a strategic partner to both the MeToo Movement and Times Up. A former national surrogate for President Obama, Wade has been an Adjunct Professor at both NYU and Rutgers. He continues to lecture on the intersections of race, sexuality, gender, and sports at universities nationally and internationally. Wade Davis graduated from Weber State University and also received an honorary Doctor of Public Service degree from Northeastern University for his leadership and ongoing efforts to eradicate homophobia and sexism in athletics.
www.wadedavis.org

Dr. Chris Donaghue, PhD, LCSW, CST
Dr. Chris Donaghue is a lecturer, therapist, educator, and author of the books *Rebel Love* and *Sex Outside the Lines: Authentic Sexuality in a Sexually Dysfunctional Culture*. He is the Director of Clinical Education for The Sexual Health Alliance, and host of both the relaunched *LoveLine* nightly radio show and *The Amber Rose Show with Dr. Chris* podcast. Dr. Donaghue practices general psychology, and specializes in individual and couples sex, relational, and marital therapy. His areas of focus include sexual and relational trauma work, sexual compulsivity, sexual dysfunctions, body image issues, body dysmorphia, body positivity, gender, and non-traditional sexuality, identities, and relationships. He works with diverse populations, including individuals of all gender expressions, sexual orientations, and Kink/BDSM/Poly experience. His office is located in Los Angeles, California.
Follow him on social @drdonaghue
www.drchrisdonaghue.com

Jamison Green is the author of numerous essays, short stories, and the book *Becoming a Visible Man* (Vanderbilt University Press, 2004/2020). He transitioned from female to male in 1988 at the age of forty and led FTM International from 1991 to 1999. He is one of the world's most accomplished activists working on trans*+ issues and has had significant influence in the areas of anti-discrimination law, employment nondiscrimination, medical education, insurance reform in the US, and access to medically necessary transgender health worldwide. He has also inspired and mentored scores of people, trans and cis, masculine, feminine, and across the gender spectrum. He is a devoted husband and the proud father of two (now adult) children.
Learn more about him at http://www.newnownext.com/jamison-green-trans-health-care-pioneer/10/2019/

Andrew Gurza is a Disability Awareness Consultant and Cripple Content Creator. In his work, he explores how the lived experience of disability *feels*, as it interplays with intersectional communities. By using hashtags like #diSAYbled, #DisabilityAfterDark, #BearinAChair and #KissAQueerCripple, Andrew shares his lived experiences of disability, queerness, sexuality and body image in a raw, vulnerable and unapologetic fashion.
Follow him on social @itsandrewgurza
www.andrewgurza.com

Jayson Moton began his yogic path in 2007. The inner drive to uplift, heal and bring a deeper sense of awareness to those who are looking for a more authentically driven life and mindset is the focus of his teaching. By extensively studying the practice of Breathwork, Kundalini Yoga and Meditation, as well as teaching it, he has witnessed his life shift and transform because of this powerful, comprehensive form of yoga. His heartwarming and uplifting classes and workshops encourage students to rediscover their own inner power, mental strength and self-awareness, while releasing and healing deep-seated blocks and unwanted stress. As a teacher, healer and guide, Jay's genuine intention has shaped and helped people establish a more compassionate, loving and profound relationship to themselves and others.
Follow him on social @jaysonmoton
www.cosmicsoulseeker.com

Kirsten King is a writer living and working in Los Angeles. She has published pieces tackling rape culture, consent, queer issues, and more in *Buzzfeed Reader, Cosmopolitan, Teen Vogue, Girlboss, INTO*, and *Huffington Post*, and in 2017 was named one of *Go Magazine's* "100 Queer Women We Love."
Follow her on Twitter @KirstenKing_

Ashlee Marie Preston is an award-winning media personality, producer and civil rights activist. She made history as the first trans woman to become editor-in-chief of a national publication and the first openly trans person to run for state office in California. Ashlee Marie was named one of The *Root 100's* "Most Influential African Americans" of 2017; profiled as one of LOGO/NewNowNext's "30 Most Influential LGBTQ Influencers" of 2017 and 2018; *PopSugar's* "Top 40 LGBTQ's" of 2017; and was listed on *OUT Magazine's* "OUT100" of 2018. In addition, she made her TED Talk debut in September of 2018 and was chosen as one of Coca-Cola's "Next Generation LGBTQ Leadership" influencers of 2018.
Follow her on social @AshleeMariePreston

Trystan Reese is a writer, storyteller, and change-maker living in Portland, Oregon. He is blessed to spend his time as partner to Biff and parent to Leo, Hailey, and Lucas.
Follow him on social @biffandi
www.trystanreese.com

Richie Reseda is a formerly-incarcerated abolitionist-feminist organizer, music and film producer, and founder of Question Culture, a social-impact record label. *Success Stories*, a transformational feminist program for incarcerated men he started while in prison, was chronicled in the CNN documentary, *The Feminist on Cell Block Y*. With Initiate Justice, an organization he co-founded with Taina Vargas-Edmond, he changed California prison policy.
Follow him on social @RichieReseda
www.questionculture.com

Mike Sagun is a certified professional men's coach and co-founder of The Unshakable Man, an organization focused on men's total health and wellness, success, purpose, and fulfillment. Mike has partnered with companies like DropBox, LinkedIn, Google, Kaiser Permanente, and Saje Wellness. He also partners with EVRYMAN, where he hosts men's groups, facilitates men's retreats, and co-leads EVRYMAN's diversity and inclusion program. When Mike isn't coaching, hosting webinars, or developing ways to help men grow, you can find him with hands dirtied from planting succulents and cacti or cooking in the kitchen with his husband, Jerry. Mike, Jerry, and their rescue pit bull, Bert, live in San Miguel de Allende, Mexico.
Follow him on social @theunshakableman and @mike.sagun
Download their *Newsletter for Men* and subscribe to their podcast at www.unshakableman.me

Cleo Stiller is a Peabody Award and Emmy Award-nominated journalist, speaker and television host on a mission to inspire positive social action around the world—and now also an author with Simon & Schuster. Stiller's book, *Modern Manhood: Conversations About the Complicated World of Being a Good Man Today*, is a #1 New Release on Amazon and has received coverage in *Fortune Magazine, Rolling Stone, ABC News, The Independent, PBS, LinkedIn's Weekend Essay*, and many more. Stiller is an Emmy-nominated and Gracie-winning journalist with a background in digital-video reporting and a passion for women's health.
Follow her on social @cleomsf
www.cleostiller.net

Jacob Tobia is an actor, writer, producer, and author of the nationally bestselling memoir, *Sissy: A Coming-of-Gender Story* (Putnam Books at Penguin Random House). Heralded by *Deadline* as an unprecedented move toward "authentic representation and inclusion," Jacob made their television debut as the non-binary character Double Trouble in Netflix's *She-Ra* and *The Princesses of Power*. From interviewing former US Presidents to giving Trevor Noah an on-air makeover on *The Daily Show*, Jacob helps others embrace the full complexity of gender and own their truth, even when that truth is messy as hell. Originally from Raleigh, North Carolina, Jacob currently lives in Los Angeles, California.
Follow them on social @jacobtobia
www.jacobtobia.com

Marquise Vilsón is an actor, award-winning activist and man of trans experience. He guest-starred in a critically acclaimed episode of LAW & ORDER: SVU, addressing the issues faced by transgender military service members. He made his New York stage debut Off-Broadway as Berta in MCC Theatre's *Charm* and his feature film debut opposite Lucas Hedges as Leon in Peter Hedges's *Ben is Back*. He has also acted in *The Kitchen*, starring Melissa McCarthy and Tiffany Haddish; NBC's *The Blacklist*; and Netflix's *Tales of the City*. As a young trans man, Marquise was featured in the 2005 documentary, *The Aggressives*, and he will executive-produce and star in the follow-up currently in production. Marquise is a long-standing and well-respected leader in New York City's ballroom scene, where he walks many categories and wins many awards as a member of the House of Balenciaga.
Follow him on social @MarquiseVilson

RECOMMENDED READING

My Gender Workbook by Kate Bornstein

As Nature Made Him by John Colapinto

Women, Race, and Class by Angela Davis

Feminism for the 99% by Nancy Fraser, Cinzia Arruzza, and Tithi Bhattacharya

Bad Feminist by Roxane Gay

Man Up: Reimagining Modern Manhood by Carlos Andres Gomez

Becoming a Visible Man by Jamison Green

The Little #MeToo Book for Men by Mark Greene

Feminism Is For Everybody by bell hooks

The Will to Change: Men, Masculinity, and Love by bell hooks

The End of Patriarchy by Robert Jensen

The Gender Knot: Unraveling Our Patriarchal Legacy by Allan G. Johnson

The Macho Paradox: Why Some Men Hurt Women and and How All Men Can Help by Jackson Katz

Men's Work: How to Stop the Violence That Tears Our Lives Apart by Paul Kivel

Redefining Realness by Janet Mock

Boys & Sex: Young Men on Hookups, Love, Porn, Consent, and Navigating the New Masculinity by Peggy Orenstein

The Descent of Man by Grayson Perry

For The Love of Men by Liz Plank

Breaking Out of the "Man Box": The Next Generation of Manhood by Tony Porter

Whipping Girl: A Transsexual Woman on Sexism and the Scapegoating of Femininity by Julia Serano

Invisible Man, Got the Whole World Watching by Mycheal Denzel Smith

Men Explain Things to Me by Rebecca Solnit

Modern Manhood: Conversations About the Complicated World of Being a Good Man Today by Cleo Stiller

Sissy: A Coming-of-Gender Story by Jacob Tobia

Cry Like a Man: Fighting for Freedom from Emotional Incarceration by Jason Wilson

RECOMMENDED VIEWING

The Aggressives by Eric Daniel Peddle

Feminist on Cell Block Y by Contessa Gayles

The Mask You Live In by Jennifer Newson

Modern Masculinity series by The Guardian

GLOSSARY

ally (noun)
A person who aligns themselves with a minority experience distinct from their own in an attempt to stand up for or fight for the rights of this class of people. A good ally knows how to listen, learn from and make room for people whose experiences have been marginalized.

binary, *also* **binary gender,** *also* **gender binary** (noun)
The notion that gender is composed of or involves only two options, i.e. men and women, and the pursuant idea that these two gender positions are opposed in character.

cis, *abbr.* **cisgender** (adjective)
Denoting or relating to a person whose sense of personal identity and gender corresponds with their assigned gender at birth, i.e., if you were assigned the male gender at birth and you identify as male, you are a cisgender man. Whereas if you were assigned female at birth and you identify as a man, you are a man of transgender experience.

emotional labor (noun)
The unpaid and unrecognized work done by members of marginalized groups to manage expectations, expressions and emotions of others not in those marginalized groups. Emotional labor is not recognized nor compensated as "real work," but it is just as exhausting and undertaken for the profit of the powerful as salaried labor in a patriarchal capitalist system is.

feminism (noun)
Advocacy of women's rights based on gender equality. Also, advocacy of universal human equality independent of gender. (See also "Intersectional Feminism.")

gender expression (noun)
The way a person visibly expresses their gender identity through appearance, dress, and behavior.

gender nonconforming (adjective)
Denoting or relating to a person whose behavior or appearance does not conform to prevailing cultural and social expectations about what is appropriate to their gender.

gender norms (noun, pl.)
The typical or standard expectations of gender. Also gender-normative or normative (adjective).

gender presentation (noun)
The way a person dresses, appears, and acts as it affects other people view their gender.

hold space, *also* **make space** (verb)
The process of witnessing or validating someone else's experience or emotional response, while also honoring your own. Think of it as creating a container to listen and observe, without judgment or defensiveness, in an effort to support, affirm and validate someone else's experience.

intersectional feminism (noun)
A term coined by legal scholar and civil rights advocate Kimberlé Crenshaw in 1989. This term is widely used now to highlight the interaction between multiple kinds of discrimination, i.e., gender, race, age, class, socioeconomic status, physical or mental ability, gender or sexual identity, religion, or ethnicity. An easy way to understand this is by picturing an intersection: intersectionality looks at the ways different types of privilege, or lack of privilege, intersect with each other.

male privilege (noun)
The social advantages given to men but not to women, transgender and non-binary people. Often privilege is not obvious to those experiencing it; people don't always notice the advantages they experience until those advantages are pointed out or taken away.

man of trans (gender) experience (noun)
A man who is assigned female gender at birth and undergoes transition to male, often involving medical assistance (which can include hormone replacement therapy and other gender-affirming procedures) to help him align his body with his identified gender.

macroaggression (noun)
Large-scale, systemic or overt aggression towards marginalized groups, i.e., violence, murder, mass incarceration, homelessness or inequitable housing opportunity, joblessness or underemployment, and so on.

microaggression (noun)
A statement, gesture, action, or incident regarded as an instance of indirect, subtle, or unintentional discrimination against members of a marginalized group such as a racial or ethnic minority.

mansplain (verb)
(Of a man) explain (something) to someone, typically a woman, often obvious, redundant or beyond the purview of the speaker, in a condescending, patronizing or insufferable manner, to the chagrin and annoyance of the listener.

mindfulness (noun)
The practice of bringing consciousness or awareness of something.

non-binary (adjective)
Denoting or related to gender identities that are outside the male-female gender binary. An assertion that gender comprises a full spectrum of identities that are not exclusively male or female, masculine or feminine.

patriarchy (noun)
A social structure in which men hold the power and women, trans people and non-binary people are largely excluded from it.

privilege (noun)
The cluster of advantages certain people or groups are given by dominant social or cultural structures.

social construct, *also* **social construction** (noun)
An idea that has been created by the people in a society an accepted, often unconsciously, as just the way things are and naturally ought to be.

toxic masculinity (noun)
Per The Good Men Project, "a narrow and repressive description of manhood, designating manhood as defined by violence, sex, status and aggression. It's the cultural ideal of manliness, where strength is everything while emotions are a weakness; where sex and brutality are yard-sticks by which men are measured, while supposedly 'feminine' traits—which can range from emotional vulnerability to simply not being hypersexual—are the means by which your status as 'man' can be taken away."

transcestors (noun, pl.)
A portmanteau fusing "transgender ancestors" or "ancestors of transgender people." People of transgender or non-binary experience who historically preceded the current generation of transgender people.

transmasculine (adjective)
A descriptive term used by those assigned female at birth who identify more strongly with masculinity than femininity.

womxn (noun, pl.)
A politically-charged feminist respelling of "women," which orthographically marks the experiential independence of womxn from men; pushes back against male-centered language; and refers com-prehensively and transhistorically to all woman-identified experience, including that of trans womxn and womxn of color.

ABOUT THE CREATOR:
Rocco Kayiatos is the creator of the *Mindful Masculinity Workbook*. He is an artist, educator, and organizer. His first album, released under the moniker Katastrophe in 2004, put him on the map as the first openly transgender man to put out an LP. He is the founding editor of the world's first trans male quarterly print journal, *Original Plumbing Magazine*, and co-editor of *Original Plumbing*: *The Best of Ten Years of Trans Male Culture* (Feminist Press, 2019). For the past six years, he put his media savvy to use as a team-leader at multiple digital-media companies, overseeing the creation of short-form viral web-series, developing and marketing content. Taking the helm of the video education department at BuzzFeed, he trained the company's interns and fellows to make viral videos in the house style. Having returned to his roots more recently, he is the proud founder of The Intentional Man Project and the co-founder and director of Camp Lost Boys, the first sleep-away summer camp exclusively for adult men of trans experience.
You can follow him on Instagram @roccokatastrophe

ABOUT THE EDITOR:
When not fingers-deep in compelling familial manuscripts, **Anastasia Kayiatos**, PhD, is a proud twin sister, a gender and Slavic Studies scholar, and a writer in her own right. Her award-winning pieces on queer performance, Deaf/disability culture, socialist wonder, and capitalist disaster have been translated into multiple languages and published in such academic journals as *Theatre Survey*, *Disability Studies Quarterly*, *Women's Studies Quarterly* and *Lambda Nordica*. She is currently on leave from things professorial and lives in the Bay Area with the most mindful man she's ever loved, Maksimka the Longhaired Chihuahua.

Cruise her profile and peruse her work (for free) on her academia.edu page, or contact her directly at akayiatos@icloud.com for assistance at any stage in the writing process, from initial conception to final copyediting. She's always on the lookout to help out with projects whose missions she can get behind.

ABOUT THE DESIGNER:
Stephanie Player is a graphic deisgner and creative director based in Los Angeles and New York. She specializes in branding, creative storytelling and engaging interactive experiences. Projects include print and web design, logo indentity design, campaigns and social media direction. She has served on the board of AIGA LA as the director of marketing, participated as a facilitator for LVMH Executive Training Program and launched Parson's School of Design's New Store Campaign. Her favorite color is leopard. She is available to collaborate.
You can follow her on Instagram @stephanie.player
www.stephanieplayer.com

ABOUT THE INTENTIONAL MAN PROJECT:
The Intentional Man Project provides men and masculine people with the skills and resources they need to embody a healthier version of maleness and masculinity. It does so virtually and in real life through meetups, online classes, workbooks, workshops, events and more. By focusing on integrity and intention while also taking a broad perspective, we strive to shift the larger definition of what it means to be a man in today's world. We are dedicated to gathering together all men— men of trans experience and cis men—to examine ourselves and our positioning in the world, and thereby create change in ourselves and our extending communities.
www.theintentionalmanproject.com